THREE BOWL
COOKBOOK

THREE BOWL
COOKBOOK

David Scott and Tom Pappas

TUTTLE PUBLISHING
Boston • Rutland, Vermont • Tokyo

First published in 2000 in the United States
by Tuttle Publishing, an imprint of Periplus
Editions (HK) Ltd., with editorial offices at
153 Milk Street, Boston, Massachusetts
02109.

Created and produced by

Carroll & Brown
20 Lonsdale Road
London NW6 6RD

Senior Managing Editor
Christina Rodenbeck

Deputy Art Director
Tracy Timson

Editors
Caroline Uzielli
Dawn Henderson

Design
Vimit Punater
Gilda Pacitti

Photography
David Murray
Jules Selmes

ISBN 0-8048-3239-0

Printed in Singapore by Tien Wah Press

First edition

06 05 04 03 02 01 00 10 9 8 7 6 5 4 3 2 1

Distributed by

USA
Tuttle Publishing
Distribution Center
Airport Industrial Park
364 Innovation Drive
North Clarendon, VT 05759-9436
Tel: (802) 773-8930
Tel: (800) 526-2778

Canada
Raincoast Books
8680 Cambie Street
Vancouver, British Columbia
V6P 6M9
Tel: (604) 323-7100
Fax: (604) 323-2600

Japan
Tuttle Publishing
RK Building, 2nd Floor
2-13-10 Shimo-Meguro, Meguro-Ku
Tokyo 153 0064
Tel: (03) 5437-0171
Fax: (03) 5437-0755

Southeast Asia
Berkeley Books Pte Ltd
5 Little road #01-01
Singapore 536983
Tel: (65) 280-1330
Fax: (65) 280-6290

Eating is basic to all beings. All beings are born, are nourished, grow old and die. In fact, monks often measured their time in the monastery by the number of meals they had eaten there.

As Zen Buddhists the appreciation of all aspects of life is of vital concern. Without that appreciation we don't experience the beneficence of the life we live every moment. These three bowls that Tom and Dave give to us are the fruit of their practice as *tenzos* (cooks)—some dishes are simple, and some complex, just like our lives.

Please give the ingredients equal care. After all the cooking is not just a matter of the best ingredients but of how much life (care, attention, zest, presence) you put into it.

Tom Pappas has been a sterling example of a tenzo at Yokoji Mountain Center and has influenced the practice of many other junior cooks. His style is somewhat unconventional, providing another facet of the great jewel of cooking.

His co-author, David Scott has been a restaurateur for 30 years, a pioneer in wholefoods and vegetarian fare, and a Zen practitioner for 18 years with a solid Zen background. His vital practice has influenced the world of cooking and the appreciation of Zen.

In a meal verse it says, "Innumerable labors brought us this food.
We should know how it comes to us."

Enjoy your three bowls and remember the whole universe has brought them to your table.

TENSHIN FLETCHER
CO-ABBOT, YOKOJI ZEN MOUNTAIN CENTER, CALIFORNIA

CONTENTS

FOREWORD

High up in the San Jacinto mountains of Southern California lies a Buddhist retreat. In the gorgeous surroundings of ancient oak and pine forest, visitors and residents follow the traditional Zen methods of seeking wisdom. Much of the day is spent in meditation and contemplation. But twice a day—at breakfast and lunch—everyone gathers for a silent meal. And the fact is, you eat well at the Zen Mountain Center.

Tom Pappas was long-time *tenzo* (cook) at the Center and his expertise and joy in the job inspired him to create these wonderful, simple meals based on Zen teaching. He has adapted Asian spirit and method to American ingredients and palates. The results are recipes that are simple and economical; healthy and delicious.

In Buddhist monasteries meals are served in three bowls—one large bowl and two smaller-sized ones. The menus in *Three Bowl Cookbook* are organized three recipes at a time—one for each bowl—and have icons that indicate which dish gets served in which of the three bowls. Normally, the large bowl holds the starch component of the meal: pasta, potatoes, or squash, for instance. One of the smaller bowls may contain a protein item, such as tofu or a combination of grains, dairy, or legumes. The other small bowl may contain a beverage, a salad or vegetable, or a fruit dessert. The three bowls together make one menu.

The three-bowl combination is designed not only to be good to eat and nutritious, but also appropriate to the season to feed both the body and the spirit. Therefore, three-bowl combinations in this book are also organized as seasonal menus. In winter, our bodies require dense, nourishing, and warm meals, while in the heat of the summer, we require lighter meals, made with fresher ingredients, and served in smaller portions. These seasonal menus are made in accordance with the ancient Chinese principles of *yin* and *yang*.

Three Bowl Cookbook is a unique guide to the wisdom, craft and pleasures of a Zen monastery kitchen. The philosophy and preparation of food are an integral part of Zen training, based upon the simple principles of love and gratitude. This is a generous and holistic way of cooking that enhances the spiritual wellbeing of all concerned.

Read, cook, enjoy.

DAVE SCOTT

Spring rains,
Summer showers,
A dry autumn.
May nature smile on us
And we will share in the bounty.

Zen and Food

To learn the way of the Buddha is to learn about oneself. To learn about oneself is to forget oneself. To forget oneself is to be enlightened by everything in the world. To be enlightened by everything is to let fall one's own body and mind.

Eihei Dogen Zenji (1200–1253)

founder of Japanese Soto Zen

Zen Buddhism was brought to Japan from China in the twelfth century by traveling monks. In Japan it flourished. A series of sages over many centuries developed and refined Zen practice, writing on all kinds of subjects including food and cooking.

In the twentieth century, Zen spread to Europe and America and it has become one of the most popular forms of Buddhism in the West. This may be because the Zen tradition is a universal one. Anyone may practice it, independent of creed.

Part of Zen's appeal lies in its essential simplicity; its emphasis on the ordinary. A Zen characteristic, and one that separates it from other paths, is that it expresses the great matters of life and death in terms of the here and now of everyday conversation and forms. The Zen practitioner seeks answers that come from our own lives, those, in Zen parlance, directly pointing at Reality. The Zen method is to demonstrate reality, not to describe it in words. Zen is above all a practical method.

Zen practitioners aspire through their training to fully express their own natures in a natural, whole, and simple way. But the essence of Zen cannot be understood or experienced through the intellect or expounded by academic argument. To get to its heart one needs personal experience and knowledge, which is gained through training techniques that have been developed over the last 1500 years.

Although details may change depending on the age, the culture, and circumstance of their teaching, the foundation of traditional Zen training is based

THE PRACTICE OF ZEN

Dogen Zenji said, "Preparing food is offering the great assembly comfort and ease." Anyone who has prepared a meal for someone they love, whether it be for family, friends or for everything that exists—as in the great assembly—may have noticed a pleasant feeling as the meal comes together. As the colors and flavors mingle with the cook's growing certainty that the meal is going to be good, something passes through the cook, through the food, through the meditation hall, and back again. I guess you would call that love.

TOM PAPPAS

on *za-zen* meditation, *koan* (enigmatic questions), *dokusan* (private interview with the teacher), and *samu* (a daily period of physical work that brings the other training methods into accord with daily life). These specifically Zen essentials operate within the Buddhist fundamentals known as the Three Treasures: Buddha, *Dharma* (teachings of the Buddha), and *Sangha* (a Buddhist community or grouping of people).

When you prepare food, do not see with ordinary eyes and do not think with ordinary mind...Do not be careless even when you work with poor materials, and sustain your effort even when you have excellent ones. If you change your attitude according to the materials, it is like varying your choice of words for different people. Then you are not a practitioner of the Way...

A refined cream soup is not necessarily better than a broth of wild grasses. When you gather and prepare wild grasses, make it equal to a fine cream soup with your true mind, sincere mind, and pure mind. This is because when you serve the assembly—the pure ocean of Buddha Dharma—you do not notice the taste of fine cream or the taste of wild grasses. The great ocean has only one taste. How much more so when you bring forth the buds of the Way and nourish the sacred body.

Eihei Dogen Zenji

In the East, Zen students who have decided to commit themselves fully to self-realization have, at least in the past, usually become monks or nuns. They have given up their worldly lives and possessions in order to follow their path under the guidance of a master within the confines of a monastic life.

In the West, Zen is much more of a lay movement. Practitioners who wish to maintain their lives both in society and in the Zen way, often find a switch of emphasis is necessary. Single-minded devotion to achieving Enlightenment or the Great Awakening has to give way to a more varied practice in which formal Zen training and the demands and concerns of ordinary life are interwoven. For instance, most people who use the Zen Mountain Center come on a retreat from their usual lives and then return, refreshed, to the hurlyburly of worldly life.

The Zen emphasis on the commonplace arises out of the understanding that, since unborn Buddha-mind is the true nature of our ordinary minds, it must follow that it can be found in ordinary life. In fact, in our very own life. This last point is most important. You don't have to be a monk to follow Zen—enlightenment is just as likely to come in the kitchen as in the meditation chamber.

A pragmatic outcome of having even partial realization of one's true or Buddha-nature is that for many it leads to a greater and more active acceptance of ordinary life and, paradoxically, a recognition of its extraordinary quality. Everyday activities, such as doing the dishes or chopping vegetables, become delightfully vested with a sense of wonder.

Although few of us have the will to devote our lives to the Buddha's path, there are legitimate ways in which all of us can introduce a little bit of enlightenment into our everyday lives—one of those ways is through cooking and eating with joy, gratitude and respect for our ingredients, our dining companions, and ourselves.

Though our modern lives are full of comfort, we have gradually become distant from our natural environment. Living in homes with heaters and air conditioners has isolated us from the changes in the four seasons. We tend to forget the gentle breeze in the tree tops and the warm rays of the sun. Shojin cooking emphasizes rather than hides these delights. On a cold and snowy day in winter, one sits hunched over, warming the tips of one's fingers on a steaming bowl of soup. And in the summer's heat there are cold noodles on a bed of ice and deep green leaves. Or one can enjoy cold, white tofu as it floats in clear water.

Soei Yoneda, Abbess, Sanko-in Temple

At the beginning of a meal, as the chant
trails off, the monk finds himself gazing
down from the meditative posture at
the day's offering. This perspective, this
settling into a feeling of hunger on the
verge of being satisfied, must be no
different now than a thousand years
ago. Rows and rows of monks, at times a
thousand strong, waited as the food
made its way through the meditation
hall—each set of bowls a different
story, a demarcation of satisfaction or
disappointment. Feelings of thanks,
entitlement, self-pity, and
dissatisfaction alternated as each monk
encountered the day's offering. Oriyoki
is an opportunity to study our most
fundamental attitudes about food.
Eating is rarely stripped down to this, its
most basic component, disassociated
from socializing, cost, or preparation.
It's simple: food suddenly appears before
us, eating occurs, and hunger is satisfied.

TOM PAPPAS

A rough translation of the Japanese word *oriyoki* is "that which contains just enough." However, in an extended sense oriyoki refers to the ceremonial use of eating-bowls during the silently taken meals in a Zen monastery. Specifically, oriyoki also refers to the actual set of nesting bowls used by each monk and received by him or her at ordination.

Originally, a single bowl was used by wandering monks in India and China and Buddhist tradition has emphasized the monk's bowl and robe as symbolic of the two things most necessary to sustain life: with one, we are supported internally (food); with the other externally (clothes, shelter). In early Buddhism, the bequest of bowl and robe was an important aspect of maintaining the line of patriarchal succession. The items were symbolic of Buddha and by using them, the patriarch emphasized Buddha's uninterrupted existence.

The present-day oriyoki sets used by Zen monks are much the same as those developed in Chinese Zen monasteries over 1000 years ago. However, an abbreviated version has now been developed in the West for lay people. It consists of three bowls as opposed to five and the largest bowl, the Buddha bowl, is free-standing rather than sitting on a wooden stand. It is this simpler set that is referred to in the title of this book.

The traditional etiquette for handling the bowls and their accompanying utensils is highly ritualized. For example, before the monks eat they raise their cloth-wrapped bowls above their heads in a gesture of respectful offering. The bowls are always held with just the thumb and first two fingers of each hand (representing the Three Treasures: Buddha, Dharma and Sangha). Sutras chanted before and after eating lend further sacred significance to the meal.

THE THREE BOWLS

Before each meal the Zen practitioner recites a sutra. There are different ones for different times of the day, season, or particular occasion, but the *Gokan No Be*, or *Five Reflections Before Eating*, is heard at most meals. This sutra is recited to remind those eating the meal of the path of the Buddha.

We offer this meal of three virtues and six tastes to the Buddha, Dharma, and Sangha and to all the life in the Dharma worlds.

First, seventy-two labors brought us this food; we should know how it comes to us.

Second, as we receive this offering, we should consider whether our virtue and practice deserve it.

Third, as we desire the natural order of mind to be free from clinging, we must be free from greed.

Fourth, to support our life, we take this food.

Fifth, to attain our Way, we take this food.

The lay person's oriyoki set

- Large Buddha bowl
- Two smaller bowls
- A wooden or metal spoon and chopsticks
- A spatula or *setsu* for bowl cleaning
- A place mat for the bowls
- A napkin, a drying cloth, and a cloth holder for the spoon

As with other spiritual paths, correct food preparation and good dietary practice form an integral part of Zen training. The philosophy of food preparation in a Zen temple is encapsulated in the style of cooking called *shojin ryori*. This may be simply translated as vegetable cooking, but shojin ryori carries with it the idea of cooking for spiritual development and its purpose is to contribute to the physical, mental, and spiritual health of the cook and partaker.

The underlying principle of shojin ryori is the very simple one of love and gratitude for the food received. Preparing and partaking of the food becomes part of daily practice and takes its place alongside other contributions to the happiness and welfare of society and ourselves. This view of food and cooking is one that can be applied in any culture and to any school of cooking.

In Japanese the word shojin is composed of the characters for "spirit" and "to progress" and the complete meaning of the word is approximately "dedication in progressing along the path of salvation." The Chinese word from which shojin was derived was itself a derivative of the Sanskrit term *virya* that contains within it the idea of both total effort and self-control, two qualities that are elemental in the Buddhist Eightfold Noble Path.

Shojin cookery has its origins in China and the philosophy underlying it was brought to Japan by monks who had been to China studying Zen. One of the most famous of these was Dogen Zenji (A.D.1200–1253) who wrote two

PHILOSOPHY OF COOKING

treatises on the subject: *A Guide for the Kitchen Supervisor* and *Instructions for the Zen Cook*. They became reference works in many Zen monasteries and the principles extolled also influenced general developments in Japanese cooking.

Zen cook and priest Keizo Kobayashi, in his book *Shojin Cookery* (The Buddhist Bookstore, San Francisco, 1977) describes how a balance of seasonal qualities is strived for by considering the five methods, the five colors, and the five flavors. These sets of five refer to the five positive roots of good spiritual practice—faith, meditation, energy, wisdom, and memory. The five methods are the different ways of preparing food: boiling, grilling, frying, steaming, and serving uncooked food. The five colors are green, yellow, red, white, and black—purple is considered black for this purpose, e.g. eggplants. The five flavors are *shoyu* or soy sauce, sugar, vinegar, salt, and spices. By balancing these three sets of five variables the Japanese Zen cook aims to make a nutritious and delicious vegetarian meal appropriate to the season.

Life itself may become a koan [a paradox] in which we try to answer the question of how to lead a life that balances our own needs with those of the people and beings around us. The buying, cooking, serving and eating of food in ways that demonstrate our appreciation of our own lives and our care for the wellbeing of other sentient beings and the natural world is a way of contributing in a satisfying and practical way to achieving this balance.

Keizo Koyabashi

In his book *Instruction for the Zen Cook*, Dogen Zenji carefully explains the qualities to look for in choosing the cook or *tenzo* for monastery duties. He says tenzo duty should be awarded only to those of excellence who exhibit faith in Buddhist teachings, have a wealth of experience and possess a righteous and benevolent heart. This is because tenzo duty involves the whole person. Further, he points out that if a person entrusted with the job of tenzo lacks such qualities or the spirit for the job, then they will endure unnecessary hardships and suffering and the work will have no value in their pursuit of the Way. The job of preparing food as far as Dogen is concerned is obviously a serious one.

The same sentiment is expressed by the Chinese monk Zongze who wrote a ten volume work called *Regulations for Zen Monasteries* (c. A.D.1102). Ten volumes! He tells the tenzo to "put your awakened mind to work, making a constant effort to serve meals full of variety that are appropriate to the need and the occasion, and that will enable everyone to practice with their bodies and minds with the least hindrance."

Another characteristic of shojin cookery is that no food should be wasted and even such things as vegetable scraps are used. The Zen cook thus needs to be skilled at both planning and cooking a meal and eliminating waste. According to Dogen, the cook should calculate down to a grain of rice how much food will be needed.

THE ROLE OF
THE COOK

A meal reflects the gentle nature and warm heart of the cook. Of course some of us are more clever with our hands than others, but if one does the best one can, a fine meal results almost as if by divine grace.

**Soei Hoshino,
Abbess of the Sanko-in Temple**

Of course, preparing food in the frame of mind recommended by Dogen and Zongze is an extremely difficult task and it requires the cook to be totally present for the job. Perhaps giving all our attention to the simplest tasks is the wisest way to start: "when washing rice focus attention on the washing and let no distraction enter."

According to the Chinese theory of yin and yang, all life flows between two opposite poles. For example, hot and cold, male and female, and heaven and earth. Everything in nature contains elements of both polarities, and the natural order arises out of a dynamic balance between the two.

The same is true of our own bodies. Our internal harmony and wellbeing depends on achieving a balance of the yin-yang polarities in all areas of our lives. This is especially so with reference to diet and the attitude of mind we bring to buying, preparing, and eating our food. Assuming the food we eat is fresh, yin foods are feminine, passive, sweet, watery, and light, while yang foods are masculine, salty, active, and heavy. A balanced diet would be neither too yang nor yin. The staples of a traditional yin-yang diet would be those of many peasant cultures—that is, grains, vegetables, legumes, nuts, seeds, and fruits. Fish and poultry are included in small amounts, with the occasional serving of red meat.

The seasons also manifest different polarities, and to maintain balance we need to eat seasonal foods. Thus, in the fall, a time of transition from the heat of the summer (yang) to the cold of the winter (yin), the cook begins to prepare more yang dishes, such as grains and poultry, while continuing to make use of seasonal fruits (yin). The darkness and coldness of winter require foods that will heat and nourish the body, such as stews, root vegetables, brown rice, buckwheat, and other grains. Mulled wine or similar warming alcoholic drinks are also appropriate in moderation. Yang power begins in the spring with the first rays of the sun. The cook now starts to lighten the diet and to slowly introduce more fresh foods and reduce servings of heavier cooked dishes. In the summer months we eat cooling foods such as salads and fruits, reduce flesh foods, and enjoy only light meals.

YIN AND YANG

Applying this yin and yang principle not only to our diets but to the rest of our lives is not something we can be taught. Instead, it is a matter of making the decision to understand how our food and lifestyle affect our physical health and mental and emotional wellbeing. To be in tune with ourselves in this way requires that we awaken our natural instincts and develop the ability to recognize what will and will not bring harmony into our lives. For most of us, this is a slow life-long process that requires patience and the desire for a more contemplative life.

How can we ever lose interest in life?
Spring has come again
And cherry trees bloom in the mountains.

Spring

FARINA WITH INDIAN SPICES

This is an interesting change of pace for hot breakfast cereal. Try serving it sprinkled with brown sugar for a delicious alternative.

INGREDIENTS
1 tablespoon butter
1 small onion, peeled and chopped
1 clove garlic, peeled and chopped
1 teaspoon curry paste
½ cup raisins
4½ cups milk
¼ cup farina (cream of wheat)
Optional: pinch of chopped fresh cilantro
Optional: ¼ cup chopped pistachios

SERVES FOUR

- Heat the butter in a large saucepan and sauté the onion and garlic.
- Once browned, add the curry paste and raisins and cook for a minute further.
- Add the milk and bring to a boil.
- Whisk in the farina and cook as instructed on the packet, then remove from the heat and transfer to a bowl.
- Serve garnished with the cilantro and pistachios, if you like.

TROPICAL FRUIT AND YOGURT

I find this dish tastes best if the fruit, yogurt and honey are barely mixed, so the honey swirls through the salad. You can use any variety of seasonal fruit.

INGREDIENTS
1 mango, peeled, seeded and chopped
1 papaya, peeled, seeded and chopped
½ pineapple, peeled and chopped
2 tablespoons raw honey
2 cups yogurt

SERVES FOUR

- Place all the chopped fruit in a bowl.
- Spoon the honey over the fruit and then add the yogurt.
- Mix lightly and serve.

26

UMEBOSHI TEA

Umeboshi *is a salty pickle, popular throughout Japan (see right). Umeboshi plum paste is available in Japanese markets and most health food stores.*

INGREDIENTS

4½ cups boiling water
1 tablespoon umeboshi plum paste

SERVES FOUR

- Place the boiling water in a saucepan, then whisk in the plum paste.
- Pour into a teapot and serve hot.

MY FIRST TASTE OF SALTED PLUM

Salty pickles are very popular in Japan. By far the most salty I've tried are the pickled plums called umeboshi.

My first taste of Zen and umeboshi occurred at a Rinzai monastery. In the Rinzai school of Zen, the first meditation period of the day starts with a bracing cup of umeboshi paste tea. Breakfast was eaten oriyoki, or formal style, with the food passed down the middle of the table. I had just arrived and was starving, so after bolting down a big bowl of exceedingly salty rice gruel, I was happy to see a bowl of what appeared to be small purple candied fruit heading my way. I helped myself to about eight of them, barely registering the looks of shock, terror and disbelief on the faces of the monks beside and across the table from me.

Even people who love umeboshi would be hard-pressed to eat more than two. That's how incredibly salty they are. The absolute shock which accompanied the first taste blew the top of my skull apart. Then each successive bite was like bringing the blade of a guillotine down on my tongue. But since it was the beginning of my first day at the monastery, I was damned if I was going to let on that these weren't the most delicious little candied purple fruits I'd ever tasted. Everyone had long-since finished eating and was sitting silently as I choked down the last umeboshi plum I was to eat for the next 12 years.

JALAPENO CORNBREAD

Cornbread is the most American of dishes, but it's a delicacy that doesn't travel well. Often, when Europeans sample their first mouthful of cornbread, their first impulse is to return their visas. Then, they begin to wonder what the baker left out of the recipe. I love it.

INGREDIENTS

Butter for greasing
1¼ cups stoneground cornmeal
½ cup all-purpose flour
1 teaspoon baking powder
1 teaspoon baking soda
1 teaspoon salt
2 teaspoons sugar
2 large eggs, beaten
2 cups buttermilk
3 tablespoons melted butter
5–6 jalapeño peppers
1 teaspoon cumin seeds

SERVES EIGHT

- Preheat oven to 450°F (230°C) and grease a 9-inch cast-iron baking pan with butter.
- Sift together the cornmeal, flour, baking powder, baking soda, salt, and sugar into a large bowl.
- In a separate bowl, whisk the wet ingredients, including the butter.
- Using tongs, hold the peppers over a gas stove flame and roast until charred. Scrape off the skin using a paring knife, then slice the peppers into small rounds. Set aside.
- Lightly toast the cumin seeds, then add them and the peppers to the wet ingredients.
- Place the greased baking pan into the preheated oven while gently folding together the wet and dry ingredients. Stir until blended—don't overmix.
- Pour this batter into the heated baking pan and bake for about 25 minutes until browned on top.
- Serve immediately, straight from the pan, cut into wedges.

FOOD FADS

I pride myself that I could, if not enjoy, at least accept even the most exotic food offerings, and I've certainly been put to the test. I was once ladling out a pot of dark stew in a Zaire convent when I noticed a monkey paw floating on the surface!

And once, in Thailand, while munching a tender fried morsel of indefinite origin, I spied a five-gallon bucket of chicken embryos behind the vendor's cart.

As a rule, I now draw the line at any recipe that employs burial as a form of cookery.

BLACK BEAN CHILI

This is a favorite at the Zen Center and a good match for Jalapeño Cornbread.

INGREDIENTS

3 cups black beans, soaked overnight
3 tablespoons olive oil
2 large onions, peeled and diced
5 cloves garlic, peeled and minced
7–8 jalapeño peppers, seeded and chopped
2 tablespoons chili powder
1 bay leaf
2 teaspoons brown sugar
2 teaspoons cumin seeds, toasted
28-ounce can whole tomatoes
1 tablespoon chopped fresh oregano
Salt and pepper to taste
¼ cup grated strong Cheddar
1 bunch chopped fresh cilantro to garnish

SERVES SIX

- Place the soaked beans in a large pot and cover with water, leaving 2 inches of water above the level of beans. Bring to a boil, then reduce the heat and simmer partially covered for 1 hour.
- Heat the olive oil in a heavy-based skillet. Add the onion and garlic. Sauté until they are softened and slightly browned.
- Then add the jalapeño peppers, chili powder, bay leaf, and sugar.
- Toast the cumin seeds in a small pan, and add them to the skillet, along with the canned tomatoes.
- Once the tomatoes have softened, mash them in the skillet with a potato masher or wooden spoon.
- Transfer the contents of the skillet to the simmering beans and add the fresh oregano. Pour in some more water if the mixture looks dry and continue simmering until the beans have completely heated through.
- Before serving, blend about 2 cups of the chili in the food processor and then return to the pot.
- Season with salt and pepper to taste.
- Top with grated Cheddar and garnish with chopped fresh cilantro to serve.

KELLY'S PEAR SALAD

INGREDIENTS

3 large, ripe pears, peeled and chopped into 1-inch cubes
1 shallot, peeled
1 tablespoon balsamic vinegar
1 tablespoon lime juice
5 tablespoons virgin olive oil
Salt and pepper
1 head green leaf lettuce, washed, dried and torn
2 heads Belgian endive, leaves removed
2 large avocados, pitted, peeled and chopped

SERVES SIX

- To make the dressing, purée one pear, the shallot, vinegar, and lime juice in a food processor.
- With the motor running, slowly drizzle in the olive oil. Season with salt and pepper, then toss with lettuce, endive, avocados, and the remaining pears.
- Serve immediately.

PAN-FRIED RISOTTO CAKES
WITH SPICY TOMATO SAUCE

Cold leftover Saffron Risotto (see page 38) is formed into round patties and fried, then topped with a simple, yet very tasty, tomato sauce.

INGREDIENTS

Enough leftover risotto to form four thick patties, about 3 cups
Cornmeal for dredging
3 tablespoons vegetable oil
2 large ripe tomatoes, chopped
2 tablespoons olive oil
¼ teaspoon crushed red pepper
Salt to taste

SERVES FOUR

- Form the cold risotto into four thick 3-inch patties and dredge in cornmeal.
- Heat the vegetable oil in a heavy-based skillet until hot, then arrange the patties in the pan. Cook them for 3–4 minutes or until browned. Then, flip them over with a spatula and cook the other side until browned.
- In a separate pan, sauté the tomatoes in the olive oil for 10 minutes. Add the red pepper and season with salt.
- Serve topped with hot tomato sauce.

Painting a Rice Cake

The paints for painting rice cakes are the same as those used for painting mountains and waters.
For painting mountains and waters, blue and red paints are used; for painting rice cakes, rice flour is used, thus they are painted in the same way and they are examined in the same way.

Dogen

WHITE BEANS WITH BASIL
AND ROASTED FENNEL

INGREDIENTS

1 cup white beans, soaked overnight
1 bay leaf
1 sprig fresh thyme
2 tablespoons olive oil
1 large bulb fennel, thinly sliced
1 small bunch basil, removed from stem and torn
Salt and pepper to taste

SERVES FOUR

- Preheat oven to 400°F (200°C).
- Place the white beans in a pot with the bay leaf, thyme, and 1 tablespoon of the olive oil.
- Cover with water, leaving 2 inches of water above the level of the beans.
- Bring to a boil, allow to reduce, and continue cooking for about 1 hour until the beans are soft.
- Meanwhile, toss the sliced fennel with the remaining olive oil and spread on a sheet pan.
- Place in the oven for 5–6 minutes until slightly browned. Then set aside.
- When the beans are cooked, drain off any excess liquid and toss with the cooked fennel and basil.
- Season with salt and pepper and serve.

WATERCRESS WITH
GARLIC

INGREDIENTS

1 tablespoon vegetable oil
2 cloves garlic, peeled and chopped
2 bunches watercress, washed and dried
1 tablespoon balsamic vinegar
Salt and pepper to taste

SERVES FOUR

- Heat the oil in a skillet or wok. Add the garlic and sauté until it just begins to turn brown.
- Then, add the watercress and stir-fry until it starts to wilt.
- Remove from heat, place into a bowl and toss with the balsamic vinegar.
- Season with salt and pepper to taste and serve.

CHANNA DAHL WITH TOMATOES

Dahl is the Hindi word for a wide variety of different legumes. Channa dahl is halved baby chickpeas, but cooks faster than chickpeas and has a rich buttery flavor and consistency. Sometimes channa dahl is difficult to find, so you can substitute any type of dahl in this recipe.

INGREDIENTS

1 cup channa dahl
1 teaspoon ground turmeric
1 teaspoon whole peppercorns
1 teaspoon cumin seeds
¼ teaspoon brown mustard seeds
1 teaspoon coriander seeds
4 jalapeño peppers, seeded and halved
3 tablespoons flaked coconut
½ cup chopped fresh cilantro
2 tablespoons butter
2 shallots, peeled and chopped
4 plum tomatoes, chopped
Salt to taste

SERVES FOUR

- Place the dahl in a saucepan and cover with water. Add the turmeric and bring to a boil.
- Reduce the heat, partially cover, and continue cooking for 1 hour or until tender. Add more water if needed.
- Carefully toast the peppercorns, cumin seeds, mustard seeds, and coriander seeds in a small, heavy-based pan. Then, crush them in a spice grinder or coffee grinder and set aside.
- Place the peppers, coconut, and cilantro in a food processor and purée to form a thick paste, then set aside.
- When the dahl is cooked, heat the butter in a large skillet.
- Add the shallots and tomatoes, sauté for a few minutes, then add the dahl and enough of its cooking liquid to cover. Bring to a boil, then simmer for 10 minutes.
- Add the ground spices and the pepper and coconut paste and mix thoroughly.
- Remove from the heat, season with salt to taste and serve.

ICED CHAI

This chilled black tea is a perfect accompaniment to these spicy dishes as it soothes and cleanses the palate.

INGREDIENTS

1 cup water
2 cinnamon sticks
5 cardamom pods
4 cloves
10 peppercorns
2-inch piece of ginger, chopped
4 cups milk
4 tablespoons black tea leaves
Honey to taste
Ice cubes to serve

SERVES FOUR

- Bring the water and all of the spices to a boil, then simmer for 10 minutes.
- Add the milk and bring back to a boil. Then, add the tea, turn off the heat, cover, and let steep for 5 minutes.
- Strain into a bowl, add the honey, and chill until cold. Serve in glasses with plenty of ice.

BASMATI RICE WITH GRILLED EGGPLANT CHUTNEY

You could make twice as much chutney and refrigerate the rest (it lasts about four days)—it's delicious spread on toasted bread. In Japan, the tender young eggplant is traditionally roasted over hot coals, but you could roast it in a hot oven for 25 minutes instead of grilling, if you prefer.

INGREDIENTS
1 cup basmati rice
1¼ cups water
½ teaspoon salt
5 or 6 Japanese eggplants, halved lengthwise
¼ cup olive oil
¼ cup red lentils
2 cloves garlic, peeled
6 jalapeño peppers, halved and seeded
1 tablespoon tamarind pulp, seeded
1 cup chopped fresh cilantro leaves
SERVES FOUR

- Cook the rice in the water with some of the salt (see page 116–117).
- Meanwhile, prepare the grill or preheat the oven to 400°F (200°C).
- Brush the halved eggplants with a little of the olive oil and grill or bake for 10 minutes or until tender and well browned. Then, remove the eggplant from the grill or oven and chop roughly. Set aside.
- Parboil the lentils for 15–20 minutes or until barely softened, then drain.
- Place the lentils, garlic, peppers, eggplant, tamarind pulp, and cilantro in a food processor and purée. With the motor running, gradually pour in the remaining olive oil.
- Spoon the mixture into a bowl and season to taste.
- Serve with the cooked rice.

MAKYO

When people start meditating, they often have visions—they see things that are not necessarily there. The Japanese word for this is makyo, and in Zen, makyo are a matter of course. When I first started to sit I saw many strange things—people turned into puppets and I conversed with Taoist immortals. Then, as I sat more, my makyo became more matter-of-fact—I spent three months tormented by a tuna-fish sandwich! It was a vegetarian monastery and, more than anything, I missed tuna. So every afternoon as I meditated I would be visited by the specter of a solid white, albacore tuna in white bread with lettuce and mayonnaise. This torturous image hung in front of my face and seemed so real, the smell and taste so pervasive, that actually eating a real tuna sandwich would have been an anti-climax.

ROASTED CINNAMON WINTER SQUASH

You can use carrots instead of squash in this dish. The original version calls for pork lard but vegetable shortening, as used here, is a decent substitute.

INGREDIENTS

1 tablespoon vegetable shortening
1–2 winter squash, peeled and cut into 1-inch-square chunks, about 5–6 cups
2 teaspoons sugar
½ teaspoon ground cinnamon

SERVES FOUR

- Preheat oven to 400°F (200°C).
- Place the vegetable shortening in a cast-iron skillet and heat in the oven.
- When the shortening is hot, add the squash and toss to cover.
- Return to the oven and cook for about 30 minutes until the squash is soft enough to pierce with a fork.
- Remove from the oven and add the sugar and cinnamon.
- Toss to coat and return the skillet to the oven for a further 10 minutes.
- Transfer the squash into a bowl and serve.

WHITE BEANS WITH FENNEL

The subtle and sweet flavor of braised fennel in garlic combines well with white beans to create a tasty dish.

INGREDIENTS

¼ pound white beans, soaked overnight
2 bay leaves
1 tablespoon olive oil
1 small onion, peeled and chopped
1 large clove garlic, peeled and minced
2 bulbs fennel, tops removed, thinly sliced
1 tomato, chopped
Salt and pepper to taste

SERVES FOUR

- Drain the beans and place them in a pot with one of the bay leaves. Add water to cover and bring to a boil.
- Continue cooking for at least 1 hour until the beans are tender, adding more water when necessary.
- Meanwhile, heat the olive oil in a heavy-based soup pot or a cast-iron skillet large enough to hold the beans.
- Add the onion and garlic to the hot oil and sauté until they begin to brown.
- Add the sliced fennel, reserving the leafy tops for garnish and continue to sauté for about 5 minutes until the fennel softens. Remove from the heat until the beans are cooked.
- Once cooked, remove the beans using a slotted spoon and add them to the fennel. Pour in enough of the bean cooking water to cover the beans and fennel and bring to a boil.
- Add the chopped tomato and the other bay leaf and cook uncovered for 15 minutes until most of the liquid is reduced.
- Season with salt and pepper, and serve garnished with chopped fennel leaves.

MASHED POTATOES WITH OLIVES AND BASIL

This is a light alternative to traditional mashed potatoes. Instead of milk or butter, an olive oil and basil pesto is used to flavor and moisten the potatoes.

INGREDIENTS

2 pounds baking potatoes, peeled and halved
1 bunch fresh basil, leaves removed from stems
½ cup virgin or extra virgin olive oil
10 Kalamata olives, pitted and cut in half
Salt and pepper

SERVES FOUR

- Place the potatoes in a large saucepan of water and boil until they are fork-tender. Drain, place back in the pan and cover so the potatoes remain hot.
- Meanwhile, purée the basil leaves and olive oil in a food processor to form a paste. Sprinkle this over the potatoes.
- Then, add the olives and season with salt and pepper to taste.
- Using a potato masher, combine the ingredients to make a rough mash.
- Add more salt and pepper, if necessary, and serve.

GOODBYE TO MY MACROBIOTIC DAYS

I used to follow a macrobiotic diet, but I only managed to keep to it for three months, before I realized that the diet was making me obsessed with food. One day I was talking to the produce delivery man at the health food store where I worked. He had been macrobiotic for many years and looked rather like a tall, gray skeleton. As we spoke, he picked up a banana and said, "You know, I haven't eaten a banana in ten years." Bananas are considered too yin for the macrobiotic diet. The thought of this man delivering fruit and vegetables day after day and never once stopping to eat a banana was too much—my macrobiotic days were over.

SLICED FRESH TOFU WITH SHOYU AND SCALLIONS

If buying tofu, try a few different brands as the taste varies. You may have the most luck in a Chinese or Japanese supermarket as the tofu will be fresher and may not be sealed in plastic.

Always keep tofu refrigerated and submerged in water, and change the water daily—tofu gets slimy as it starts to go bad. It's often graded from soft to extra-firm, indicating the amount of water that was squeezed out of it during its preparation. Extra-firm is good for stir-frying and a less firm variety is more tasty when eaten raw.

INGREDIENTS
10-ounce block of tofu
Shoyu (soy sauce) to taste
3 tablespoons chopped scallions
SERVES FOUR

- Rinse the tofu well, dry on a paper towel and slice into bite-sized pieces.
- Arrange in a bowl and serve topped with the shoyu and scallions.

SEA GREENS WITH CUCUMBER AND AVOCADO

Wakame is a seaweed used widely in Japanese cooking. It's available in most health food stores or Japanese markets.

INGREDIENTS
2 ounces dried wakame
3 tablespoons rice vinegar
½ tablespoon sugar
1 teaspoon sake
¼ teaspoon salt
1 teaspoon lime juice
1 avocado, pitted, peeled and chopped
1 cucumber, peeled, seeded and chopped
SERVES FOUR

- Reconstitute the wakame in cool water for 15 minutes, rinse and chop well.
- Add the wakame to a small pan of boiling water and cook for 5 minutes.
- Drain and spread onto a plate to cool.
- To make the dressing, whisk the vinegar, sugar, sake, salt, and lime juice in a bowl.
- Pour over the wakame. Toss in the avocado and cucumber, and serve.

TOFU

Of the Western chefs I've known, I've never come across one who will even touch tofu. Why this prejudice? Maybe it's due to the Western assumption that tofu is first and foremost a meat substitute. Chinese and Japanese chefs go through many arcane procedures to make tofu act and taste like meat, but I would guess that ultimately they love tofu for just being tofu. At the Zen Center I make my own tofu (see recipe on page 119). Served with shoyu and scallions, the taste of warm, fresh sliced tofu is unique and intoxicating.

UDON NOODLES WITH PEANUT SAUCE

This peanut sauce is an old standby at the Zen Center—it can be made quickly using many variations of ingredients and kept in the refrigerator for up to two days.

INGREDIENTS

1 pound udon *noodles*
1-inch piece of ginger, peeled
4 cloves garlic, peeled
4–5 jalapeño peppers, seeded
4 scallions, cleaned and roughly chopped
½ cup chopped fresh cilantro
1 cup peanut butter, unsalted
¼ cup rice vinegar
2 tablespoons shoyu *(soy sauce)*
½ lime, juiced
2 tablespoons sugar
2 tablespoons toasted sesame oil
1 cup bean sprouts

SERVES FOUR

- Cook the udon noodles according to the packet instructions.
- Place the ginger, garlic, peppers, scallions, and cilantro in a food processor and lightly purée with a few short bursts.
- Add the remaining ingredients, except the bean sprouts, and purée well.
- If the sauce seems too thick to toss with pasta, add a little water. If it's too thin, add a little more peanut butter.
- Toss the sauce with the warm noodles or chill and toss with noodles that have been submerged in cold water and drained.
- Top with the bean sprouts and serve either hot or cold.

Zen and Work

One day without work is a day without food.

Zen Proverb

SAFFRON RISOTTO

*Risotto is an Italian dish employing a
unique cooking technique and
a short-grain rice called arborio.
It is simmered to completion
uncovered. I'd recommend doubling
the recipe so you have enough to make
Pan-Fried Risotto Cakes with the
leftovers (see page 30).*

INGREDIENTS

2 tablespoons butter or olive oil
2 shallots, peeled and chopped
¼ teaspoon saffron threads
1½ cups arborio rice
½ cup dry white wine
6–7 cups vegetable stock
¼ cup freshly grated Parmesan cheese plus a little extra to garnish
Salt and pepper to taste

SERVES FOUR

- Heat the butter or oil in a large heavy-based skillet or saucepan.
- Add the shallots and saffron, sauté for a few minutes then add the rice.
- Stirring continuously, heat the rice for about 5 minutes, then add the wine.
- Simmer until the wine is absorbed.
- Begin to add the stock; about 1 cup at a time. I usually have the vegetable stock heated in a pot on the stove so it's easy to ladle into the rice.
- Cook, stirring constantly, until each cup of stock is absorbed before adding the next.
- Taste after 15–20 minutes. The rice should be soft but not mushy. If the rice has absorbed all the stock you have on hand but still isn't cooked, add hot water. When finished, the rice should have a creamy consistency—leave the rice a little moister than you would serve it because it will continue to absorb the liquid as it cools.
- Remove from heat and stir in the Parmesan cheese.
- Add the salt and pepper to taste and garnish with shavings of Parmesan cheese. Serve immediately.

1 small red onion, peeled and chopped

2 jalapeño peppers, seeded and finely chopped

1 lime, juiced

¼ cup fresh cilantro, chopped

2 plum tomatoes, chopped

2 tablespoons olive oil

Salt and pepper to taste

SERVES FOUR

CORN AND BLACK BEAN SALAD

Cook the beans to whatever tenderness suits your own taste, but they shouldn't be so mushy that they can't maintain their shape and color when tossed with the other ingredients. Rinsing the beans in water slows down the cooking time and gives the beans a mid-point wash so they will look great in the salad.

INGREDIENTS

1 cup black beans, soaked overnight or softened in a pressure cooker (you may substitute canned beans, if necessary)

1 bay leaf

4 ears of fresh corn

1 red bell pepper, roasted, peeled and seeded

- Simmer the beans in ample cooking water with the bay leaf for 30 minutes.
- Remove from the heat and drain.
- Rinse with cold water.
- Return the beans to the pot, cover with cold water and cook for about 20 minutes or until tender.
- Meanwhile, slice the kernels from the corn and place in a seasoned cast-iron pan. Cook, stirring constantly, until the kernels begin to brown.
- Put the corn in a bowl and toss with the roasted pepper, red onion, jalapeños, lime juice, fresh cilantro, tomatoes, and olive oil.
- Drain the beans, add to the rest of the ingredients, and toss together.
- Season with salt and pepper and serve.

RADICCHIO WITH SUMMER SAVORY VINAIGRETTE

INGREDIENTS

1 shallot, peeled and finely chopped

1 tablespoon summer savory, finely chopped

1 tablespoon balsamic vinegar

½ teaspoon salt

2–3 tablespoons extra virgin olive oil

2 heads radicchio, washed, dried and torn

1 ripe tomato, sliced

A handful of pitted black olives

Ground black pepper

SERVES FOUR

- Combine the shallot, savory, vinegar, and salt in a wooden salad bowl.
- Whisk in some olive oil to your taste.
- Add the other ingredients and toss.

SPICY SQUASH STEW
WITH PEPPERS

You can use any variety of pepper
you choose for this stew, so learn to
experiment. With hot peppers, the
best way to find out how many to
use is to slice off a piece and taste it.

INGREDIENTS

4 cups water or vegetable stock
⅓ cup red lentils, rinsed
1½ tablespoons olive oil
1 small onion, peeled and diced
2 cloves garlic, peeled and minced
1 carrot, peeled and diced
1 butternut squash, peeled, seeded and cut into small chunks, 4–5 cups
14-ounce can of whole tomatoes
1 Scotch bonnet or 2 jalapeño peppers, seeded and minced
Salt and pepper to taste
½ cup chopped fresh cilantro
½ lime, juiced

SERVES FOUR TO SIX

- Heat the water or stock in a soup pot. Add the lentils and bring to a boil. Reduce the heat and simmer, partially covered, for 30 minutes.
- Meanwhile, heat the oil in a heavy-based skillet and sauté the onion, garlic, and carrot for 2–3 minutes.
- Add the squash and sauté for about 5–10 minutes until it begins to soften.
- Transfer to the soup pot and add the canned tomatoes with the juice. (Crush them before they go into the soup to help the cooking process.)
- Bring to a boil again, then reduce to a simmer for 35–45 minutes.
- Add the pepper or peppers and simmer for a further 10 minutes.
- Using a potato masher, lightly crush together part of the stew. The goal isn't to purée it, just to mingle the flavors.
- Taste for spiciness and season with salt and pepper. Serve garnished with cilantro and a sprinkle of lime juice.

STEPPING STONES

People often say to me, " I'm not a
good cook because I can't make
everything come out at once." What's
important is to be able to see all the
necessary steps laid out beforehand like
stepping stones. And immerse yourself
in each individual task, taking one step
at a time—that's attention to detail.
With practice it all flows, even
confusion, and soon you'll be
doing it naturally.

TAMARIND MASHED POTATOES WITH COCONUT MILK AND CUMIN

INGREDIENTS

2 pounds Idaho potatoes, peeled and cut into chunks
¼ teaspoon salt
1 cup coconut milk
2 tablespoons tamarind pulp, seeded
1 dried chili pepper
1 tablespoon sugar
1 stalk lemon grass, chopped
2 tablespoons butter
1 teaspoon brown mustard seeds
1 teaspoon cumin seeds
½ cup chopped fresh cilantro

SERVES FOUR

- Cook the potatoes in a saucepan of boiling salted water.
- Meanwhile, heat the coconut milk in a small saucepan along with the tamarind, chili, sugar, and lemon grass. Bring to a boil, then reduce the heat and leave on a simmer.
- When the potatoes are fork-tender, drain and place in a bowl.
- Strain the simmering coconut milk mixture, making sure the tamarind has liquefied.
- Pour over the potatoes and mash using a potato masher.
- Meanwhile, gently heat the butter in a small saucepan and add the mustard and cumin seeds; be careful not to burn them.
- Once the mustard seeds begin to pop, tip them over the mashed potatoes.
- Garnish with the cilantro and serve immediately.

AVOCADO AND BUTTER LEAF SALAD

INGREDIENTS

1 lime, juiced
2 teaspoons shoyu (soy sauce)
Approximately 2–3 tablespoons olive oil
1 tablespoon minced fresh dill
2 avocados, pitted, peeled and sliced
1 head butter leaf lettuce, washed and dried
Freshly ground pepper to taste

SERVES FOUR

- In a salad bowl, mix together the lime juice and shoyu.
- Gradually whisk in the olive oil until the liquid is slightly thickened.
- Add the dill and avocado slices.
- Before serving, toss with the lettuce and season with freshly ground pepper to taste.

FETA SPAGHETTI

"If I were to choose my last meal, it would be spaghetti with feta cheese." My father makes this declaration whenever he prepares this dish which combines the flavors of garlic, olive oil and pungent feta cheese.

INGREDIENTS

1 pound dried spaghetti
3 tablespoons olive oil
4 cloves garlic, peeled and minced
1 cup feta cheese, crumbled
Handful of fresh parsley, chopped

SERVES FOUR

- Cook the pasta until al dente (see page 117).
- Meanwhile, heat the olive oil in a small skillet. Add the minced garlic and sauté until it begins to brown.
- Then, remove the skillet from the heat and set aside.
- Once the pasta is cooked, drain it thoroughly and transfer it to a serving bowl.
- Add the feta cheese and parsley to the olive oil and garlic in the skillet and then toss with the hot spaghetti.
- Serve immediately.

LAST MEALS

I'm not sure how the tradition of offering condemned prisoners a last meal started, but looking over a list of notorious killers' last requests, I'm struck by the poignancy these dishes take on when viewed in this context.

For example, one prisoner ordered coffee, eggs, bacon, fried chicken, mashed potatoes and steak pie. I imagine this meal would usually be eaten at dawn, so eggs, bacon and coffee are perfectly natural requests. Then, as if wishing to encompass one more whole day on earth, the prisoner also wanted fried chicken, mashed potatoes, and steak pie!

I find this list compelling and I begin to consider how it must taste. Then I try to imagine the cook who prepared that sacred meal. I see him alone in the early morning kitchen gazing at that list of strangely grouped entrées, then quietly going about constructing the meal.

SHREDDED CARROT AND
APPLE SALAD

*This quick and simple salad will keep
for a few hours in the refrigerator.*

INGREDIENTS
1 apple, peeled and cored
4 carrots, peeled
½ lemon, juiced
1 tablespoon dried currants
½ jalapeño pepper, seeded and minced
½ teaspoon lightly toasted cumin seeds
Salt to taste
Optional: 1 tablespoon toasted pine nuts
SERVES FOUR

- Grate the apple and then the carrots
  into a bowl. Add the lemon juice and
  toss to cover.
- Add the currants, pepper, and cumin,
  and toss together with the salt. Mix in
  the pine nuts, if desired, and serve.

FRESH MINTED
LEMONADE

*A bowl of fresh squeezed lemonade
cuts through the strong flavor of garlic
in the Feta Spaghetti dish.*

INGREDIENTS
5–6 fresh mint leaves, minced
¼ pound sugar
4 lemons, juiced
5 cups water
SERVES FOUR

- In a bowl, or in a mortar with a pestle,
  crush the mint and sugar; this releases
  the flavor of the mint leaves.
- Place the mixture into a pitcher with
  the lemon juice, then stir in the water.
- Serve cold.

A SIMPLE RASAM

Rasam is a simple South Indian soup. This lemony version goes well with the southwestern spices of the other bowls.

INGREDIENTS

½ cup red lentils, rinsed
½ teaspoon turmeric
2 tomatoes, chopped
2–3 jalapeño peppers, seeded and chopped
1-inch piece ginger, peeled
1-inch ball of tamarind, seeds removed
2 cloves garlic, peeled
2 teaspoons butter
1 teaspoon brown mustard seeds
1 lemon, juiced
Salt and freshly ground pepper
Handful fresh cilantro to taste

SERVES FOUR

- Cover the lentils with water in a saucepan and bring to a boil.
- Add the turmeric and chopped tomato and simmer for 45 minutes.
- Then, purée the peppers, ginger, tamarind, and garlic cloves in a food processor and add to the cooked lentils. Cook for another 20 minutes.
- Meanwhile, melt the butter in a small saucepan and add the mustard seeds. Cook the seeds until they begin to pop.
- Add the mustard seeds to the soup, along with the lemon juice.
- Season to taste with salt, a generous amount of freshly ground pepper, and some fresh cilantro.
- Serve immediately.

FRIED OKRA WITH HOMEMADE PEPPER SAUCE

Homemade Pepper Sauce can be prepared a few days ahead of time. This dish works best with fresh tender okra—if the okra is too fibrous, it won't benefit from this quick-frying method.

INGREDIENTS

5 plum tomatoes
1 red onion, peeled and quartered
3 jalapeño peppers, sliced in half and seeded
1–2 dried red peppers or an ancho pepper, seeded
1–2 tomatillos (if available)
Salt to taste
Fresh cilantro and lime juice to taste
20–30 okra pods, washed and dried
1 cup buttermilk
1 cup cornmeal seasoned with salt and pepper
2 cups vegetable oil for frying

SERVES FOUR

- For the pepper sauce, combine the tomatoes, red onion, jalapeños, dried

MASHED POTATOES
WITH BUTTERMILK AND
TOASTED CUMIN

red peppers, and tomatillos in a large cast-iron pan.

- Dry-roast over medium heat for 20 minutes, tossing occasionally with a spatula. The tomatoes should begin to blacken and cook along with the peppers and onion.
- Once all the vegetables are slightly blackened, transfer them to a food processor and purée until smooth. Set aside and allow to cool. Then season to taste with salt, cilantro, and lime juice.
- To prepare the okra pods, dip into the buttermilk and dredge in the seasoned cornmeal.
- Heat the oil in a heavy-based skillet and drop the dipped okra pods into it. Cook until the okra become golden brown. Remove the okra and place on a paper towel to drain.
- Place the cooked okra onto a serving plate and top with the pepper sauce.

Here's a southwestern variation on traditional mashed potato that is comparatively low in fat. This dish can be reheated in the oven in a covered baking dish.

INGREDIENTS
2 pounds russet potatoes, peeled and quartered
⅔ cup buttermilk
2 tablespoons olive oil
1½ teaspoons cumin seeds
Salt and pepper to taste
A few sprigs of fresh cilantro for garnish
SERVES FOUR

- Boil the potatoes in salted water for about 20 minutes until fork-tender.
- Drain, then return them to the pot and heat uncovered for a few minutes on a low flame—this will get rid of any excess water.

- Next, mash the potatoes with the buttermilk and olive oil, or alternatively purée them in a food processor.
- Toast the cumin seeds in a small heavy-based skillet, being careful not to burn them.
- Add the toasted cumin seeds to the mashed potatoes and season with salt and pepper.
- Garnish with fresh cilantro.
- Serve immediately or set aside to be reheated later.

The willows are in full bloom!
I want to pile up the blossoms
Like mountain snow.

Summer

KOKYO'S REAL SWISS MUESLI

Muesli should be prepared the night before, so that the oats are softened by the morning. Any kind of dried fruit or nuts can be added to the basic recipe below—you decide.

INGREDIENTS

½ lemon, juiced
2 apples, peeled and cored
1½ cups rolled oats
½ cup raisins or currants
⅓ cup sliced almonds
¾ cup plain yogurt
Honey or maple syrup to taste

SERVES FOUR

- Pour the lemon juice into a small bowl and grate the apples into it. Toss to coat the apples in the juice.
- Now add the oats, raisins, almonds, yogurt, and sweetener.
- Mix together thoroughly, then cover and refrigerate overnight.
- The next morning, taste the muesli and adjust the flavors if necessary.
- Serve chilled or at room temperature.

The One in the Shrine

A monk asked, "What is Buddha?"
The Master replied, "The one
in the shrine."
The monk protested, "But isn't the
one in the shrine a clay
figure made from mud?"
"Yes, that's right," said the Master.
"Then what is Buddha?"
asked the monk.
The Master again said, "The one
in the shrine."
The monk asked, "What is
my self-being?"
The Master replied, " Have
you had your breakfast?"
The monk replied, "Yes, I have."
The Master said, "Then wash
your bowl."
All of a sudden, the monk was
enlightened.

The Record of Chou-Chou

Translated by James Green

48

WARM FRUIT COMPOTE

This is a quick and very delicious version of stewed fruit.

INGREDIENTS
2 tablespoons butter
2 large apples, peeled and chopped
1 pear, peeled and chopped
6 prunes, chopped
6 dried apricots, chopped
1 cinnamon stick
2 teaspoons sugar
2 teaspoons lemon juice
SERVES FOUR

- Melt the butter in a heavy-based skillet. Add the apples, pear, prunes, apricots, and cinnamon stick.
- Sauté, stirring often, until the fruit has completely softened.
- Add the sugar and continue to sauté for a further couple of minutes.
- Remove from the heat, sprinkle with the lemon juice and serve warm.

MINDFUL CHOPPING

Sometimes I work with people new to Zen who chop an onion in what they imagine is a mindful, Zen way; slow and oblivious. In contrast, I've watched professional cooks drunk out of their minds working quickly and efficiently and I've seen cooks with debilitating anger and terrible attitudes toward the people around them, yet they seem to be good at what they're doing.

CHAI

Chai is a spiced black tea, sweetened with honey and brewed with milk.

INGREDIENTS
1 cup water
2 cinnamon sticks
5 cardamom pods
4 cloves
10 peppercorns
2-inch piece of ginger, peeled and chopped
4 cups milk
3½ tablespoons black tea leaves
Honey to taste
SERVES FOUR

- Bring the water and all spices to a boil in a saucepan.
- Simmer for about 10 minutes.
- Add the milk and bring back to a boil. Add the tea, then turn off the heat, cover and let the mixture steep for 5 minutes.
- Strain into a teapot, add the honey to taste, and serve hot.

SIMPLE TOMATO SAUCE
WITH PASTA

A sauce like this depends on the quality of the tomatoes. It's good to have on hand a tube of tomato paste in case the flavor needs a little more intensity. If the tomatoes aren't quite ripe, adding 1–2 teaspoons of sugar helps to reduce the acidity. If you try to make this sauce from the hard, pale tomatoes often found at supermarkets, it will be a lost cause. If you can't find good quality tomatoes, use the canned varieties.

As for the garlic, it's amazing how much you can put in without it being overpowering—especially if it's browned properly. Don't mince the garlic ahead of time as it quickly loses its flavor—I've never tried the jailhouse method depicted in the movie Goodfellas *where the garlic is sliced paper-thin with a razor blade! The most important thing about the garlic is not to burn it during cooking.*

INGREDIENTS

1 pound pasta
4 large tomatoes, peeled and seeded
3 tablespoons olive oil
3–5 large cloves garlic, peeled and minced
Salt, pepper, and sugar to taste
Handful of fresh basil leaves, torn
Optional: pinch of cayenne

SERVES FOUR

- Cook the pasta until al dente (see recipe on page 117).
- Bring another pot of water to a boil.
- To peel the tomatoes, score their undersides with a shallow "x" and drop them into the boiling water for about 1 minute. Remove the tomatoes, then peel off and discard the skin.

- Next, cut the peeled tomatoes in half horizontally, so that you can easily squeeze out the seeds and juice.
- Discard the seeds and reserve the juice. Then, chop up the meat of the tomatoes and set aside.
- Heat the oil in a pan and add the garlic. Sauté until nut brown. Beware: the garlic goes from perfect to burnt alarmingly quickly.
- Add the tomatoes and simmer for a while depending on how well cooked

you want the sauce—the longer the tomatoes are cooked, the thicker and more flavorsome the sauce. Add the reserved tomato juice or a little water if the sauce becomes too thick.

- Add the salt, pepper, and a pinch of sugar to taste. Throw in the fresh basil, torn—cutting with a knife blackens the leaves.
- Toss with hot cooked pasta and add a pinch of spicy cayenne if desired.
- Serve immediately.

RAPINI WITH BALSAMIC VINEGAR

Rapini is a popular Italian vegetable that looks like leafy broccoli and tastes like spicy mustard greens.

INGREDIENTS
2 bunches rapini, ends of stems removed
Spray of virgin olive oil
Salt and pepper to taste
Balsamic vinegar to taste
SERVES FOUR

- Boil or steam the rapini until just tender. Then drain and spread it evenly on a platter.
- Spray the rapini with the virgin olive oil, then sprinkle with salt, pepper, and balsamic vinegar.
- Serve immediately.

BROILED FIGS WITH GORGONZOLA AND HONEY

This recipe can be made using raw ripe figs but the broiling adds warmth and flavor which complements Gorgonzola and honey. For more richness, you could grill the figs on an oiled grate over hot coals.

INGREDIENTS
12 ripe figs
1 cup Gorgonzola cheese, crumbled
Raw honey
SERVES FOUR

- Heat up the broiler.
- Slice the ripe figs in half, place them face down in a cast-iron skillet and place them under the hot broiler until browned.
- When the figs are brown on one side, gently turn them over and broil the other side for a further couple of minutes until browned.
- Remove the figs from the skillet and place them in a bowl.
- Sprinkle with Gorgonzola, drizzle with raw honey, and serve immediately.

PASTA WITH AVOCADO SAUCE

You can prepare the avocado sauce ahead of time and then toss it with the fresh, hot pasta to stir up the flavors.

INGREDIENTS

1 pound pasta—choose one with a fancy shape such as farfalle
1 ripe avocado, pitted, peeled and chopped
½ lemon, juiced
½ jalapeño pepper, seeded and chopped
1–2 ripe tomatoes, seeded and chopped
1 clove garlic, peeled and minced
10 fresh basil leaves, torn
¼ cup extra virgin olive oil
Salt and pepper to taste

SERVES FOUR

- Cook the pasta until al dente (see recipe on page 117)
- In a large bowl, mix the avocado, lemon juice, jalapeño, tomatoes, garlic, basil, and olive oil.
- Toss with the pasta, season, and serve.

MARSHMALLOW MEMORIES

It's often said that before you practice Zen, mountains are just mountains and rivers are just rivers. Then in the course of practice, you become aware that mountains aren't really mountains and rivers are no longer rivers. But supposedly, after enlightenment is fully manifest, mountains are just mountains, and rivers just rivers.

When I was a boy I loved peanut butter and marshmallow fluff sandwiches. To me the sweet and salty flavors and the creamy and glutinous textures were the absolute apex of culinary perfection. One Saturday morning, while my mother was asleep, my sister and I commandeered the kitchen with our sights set on unlimited access to the aforementioned substances. This was probably my first solo venture into the culinary arts and I rose to the occasion, immediately parting with tradition, with the heretical suggestion that we introduce a layer of chocolate syrup between the peanut butter and marshmallow. My sister gave her assent but I still remember those feelings of misgiving and dread which go hand in hand with messing with perfection. Half way through eating the new sandwich, I was already craving the original peanut butter and marshmallow sandwich.

Years later, as a college freshman, I rushed to the supermarket and purchased the holy trinity of bread, peanut butter, and marshmallow. It's hard to say exactly what it was I was looking for that day, but any hopes of capturing memories of a simpler, sunnier time were dashed by my first bite. It tasted awful. Twenty years passed and I forgot about marshmallow fluff until one day at the Zen Center when four jars mysteriously appeared in the kitchen. It seems a group of Tibetan Buddhists had covered the altar with white food offerings in honor of Avalokitesvara, the goddess of compassion. So there were popcorn, hard-boiled eggs, and Tic-Tacs, and of course the hallowed fluff. I immediately made myself a sandwich and this time it tasted great.

So in the beginning, marshmallow fluff was just marshmallow fluff. Then for a time it wasn't, but in the end, marshmallow fluff was just marshmallow fluff. And it's good.

ROASTED CORN AND PEPPER SALAD

INGREDIENTS

6 ears of fresh corn
1 tablespoon olive oil
1 jalapeño pepper, seeded and chopped
1 small red onion, peeled and chopped
1 small red bell pepper, seeded and chopped
½ lime, juiced
½ teaspoon cumin seeds, toasted
1 tablespoon chopped fresh cilantro
Salt and pepper to taste

SERVES FOUR

- Scrape the kernels from the corn. Hold the corn upright with a fork, then cut between the cob and the kernels using a sharp knife.
- Heat the oil in a heavy-based skillet.
- Add the corn and sauté for 30 seconds.
- Then add the jalapeño, onion, and red pepper and sauté for a further 5 minutes. Transfer to a bowl.
- Add the lime juice, toasted cumin seeds, and cilantro. Season with salt and pepper, mix thoroughly, and serve.

PARSLIED CARROTS

INGREDIENTS

5 large carrots, peeled and cut into chunks
1 shallot, peeled and finely chopped
1 tablespoon butter or olive oil
1 tablespoon chopped fresh parsley
1 tablespoon chopped fresh dill
Salt and pepper to taste

SERVES FOUR

- Steam the carrots for about 8 minutes until tender.
- Transfer the steamed carrots to a bowl and toss with the shallot, butter or oil, parsley, and dill.
- Season with salt and pepper to taste and serve.

The Cook Held Up a Vegetable Leaf

*The Master asked the cook,
"For today's meal, will it be raw
vegetables or cooked vegetables?"
The cook held up a vegetable leaf.
The Master said, "Those who know
kindness are few, those
who abuse kindness are many."*

The Record of Chou-Chou

Translated by James Green

QUINOA TABBOULEH

Quinoa was the grain of choice of the Aztecs and Mayans. It's not as widely available today, but you can usually find it at health food stores. If not, you may use the more traditional bulgur wheat, but quinoa has a lighter, more interesting texture and flavor.

INGREDIENTS
1 cup quinoa
2 cups water
½ teaspoon salt
1 lemon, juiced
¼ cup olive oil
1 cucumber, peeled, seeded and chopped
1 red onion, peeled and chopped
¼ cup chopped fresh parsley, chopped
¼ cup chopped fresh mint
½ cup feta cheese
½ cup Kalamata olives, pitted
Salt and pepper
SERVES FOUR

- Rinse the quinoa thoroughly in a fine mesh strainer. Drain and place it in a heavy-based skillet. Heat, stirring constantly until the grains separate and begin to brown. (I usually cook quinoa without using oil but then toss olive oil into the cooked grain later on.)
- Add the water and the salt and bring to a boil. Then, reduce the heat and cook for about 15 minutes until the liquid is absorbed.
- Transfer to a bowl and set aside to cool.
- Whisk together the lemon juice and 1 tablespoon of the olive oil in a small bowl. Set aside.
- Place the remaining oil, the cucumber, onion, parsley, and mint in a separate, larger bowl, add the quinoa and the lemon and oil dressing and toss.
- Sprinkle with the feta cheese and pitted Kalamata olives.
- Season with salt and pepper to taste and serve.

SWEET SAUTEED CHERRY TOMATOES

This dish goes extremely well with the Quinoa Tabbouleh. If you can't find cherry tomatoes, you can use the larger variety of tomato.

INGREDIENTS

4 cups cherry tomatoes or about 4 cups large ripe tomatoes
¼ cup olive oil
2 tablespoons sugar

SERVES FOUR

- Wash and dry the tomatoes. If using large tomatoes, cut them in half and discard the seeds and juice, then chop them into cherry-sized pieces.
- Heat the oil in a heavy-based saucepan until hot, but be careful not to burn it.
- Add the tomatoes and toss.
- Then add the sugar and continue cooking for 2–3 minutes.
- Transfer into a serving dish and serve immediately.

BASIL HUMMUS

INGREDIENTS

1½ pounds dried chickpeas or channa dhal (baby chickpeas), soaked and drained
2 cloves garlic, peeled
1 large lemon, juiced
¼ cup olive oil
2 cups fresh basil leaves, washed and dried
Salt and pepper to taste

SERVES FOUR

- Boil the chickpeas in a saucepan for about 1 hour. Drain, reserving the cooking liquid.
- Purée the garlic and chickpeas in a food processor. Add the lemon juice, then slowly pour in the olive oil and some cooking liquid, if it seems dry.
- Add the basil, then season, and serve.

BREAD SALAD WITH
TOMATOES AND HERBS

This is a great solution for getting rid of slightly stale bread. It should be made a few hours ahead of time to enable the flavors to blend.

INGREDIENTS

Spray of olive oil

½ teaspoon fresh rosemary, finely chopped

---

1 loaf crusty Italian or sourdough bread, chopped into 1-inch pieces

---

8 Kalamata olives, pitted and chopped

½ cup fresh basil or parsley, chopped

---

1 teaspoon fresh oregano or savory, chopped

½ red onion, peeled and chopped

---

4 large ripe tomatoes

½ cup extra virgin olive oil

½ lemon, juiced

---

2 tablespoons wine vinegar

Salt and pepper to taste

SERVES FOUR

- Preheat oven to 400°F (200°C). Spray a sheet pan with the olive oil and then sprinkle it well with the chopped rosemary.
- Arrange the bread on the sheet pan, and then spray again with olive oil.
- Bake in the oven for 10–15 minutes until the bread begins to brown. Remove and allow to cool.
- Meanwhile, mix together the olives, basil, oregano, and red onion.
- Halve the tomatoes. Squeeze out and discard the juice and seeds.
- Roughly chop the tomato meat and then add to the other ingredients.
- When the bread has cooled, mix with the tomato and olive mixture.
- Drizzle over the olive oil, lemon juice, and vinegar and season with salt and pepper to taste.
- Cover and allow the salad to rest at room temperature for at least 2 hours before serving.

FLYING SAUCEPAN
While preparing the midday meal at the Center one day, the cooks were startled when a huge pan fell from its hook, landing on the steel work table with a crash. When the commotion died down a cook asked, "Anyone get enlightened?"

GRILLED JAPANESE EGGPLANT

If at all possible, the eggplants should be prepared on a small charcoal grill, but they can also be roasted in a hot oven. You could cook some extra eggplant and make Grilled Eggplant Chutney (see recipe on page 33) to accompany the meal or to keep for another time.

INGREDIENTS

2 cloves garlic, peeled
1 tablespoon olive oil
6 Japanese eggplants, sliced in half lengthwise
Salt and lemon juice to taste

SERVES FOUR

- Prepare the grill or preheat oven to 400°F (200°C).
- Crush the garlic into a bowl and mix with the olive oil.
- Brush the garlic mixture over the cut surfaces of the eggplant halves and sprinkle each half with salt.
- If grilling, place the eggplant face down on a clean grate once the coals are glowing. Cook them until well browned. Then, flip the eggplants over and grill until the other side is well browned. (Or roast in the preheated oven for 15 minutes each side.)
- Remove the eggplants from the heat and slice them into bite-sized pieces.
- Sprinkle with salt, drizzle with the lemon juice and serve.

TZATZIKI

Greek yogurt is made from sheep or goat milk and is unbelievably rich and thick. If you can't find it, you could use regular yogurt which has been left to sit in a mesh sieve or a coffee filter to lose some of its water.

INGREDIENTS

1 large cucumber, peeled, seeded and finely chopped
2 cloves garlic, peeled and minced
1 tablespoon fresh dill, chopped
2½ cups Greek yogurt
Salt and pepper to taste
1 tablespoon extra virgin olive oil

SERVES FOUR

- Mix together the garlic, dill, and yogurt in a large bowl. Add the chopped cucumber, salt and pepper, then drizzle with the olive oil.
- Set aside for at least 1 hour, then taste.
- Adjust the seasoning and serve.

FRIED RICE

This is an old standby for getting rid of cold leftover rice. It's great for breakfast and the amount of egg used can be varied. If you use more egg, you get a sort of rice omelet.

INGREDIENTS

1 tablespoon peanut or vegetable oil
1 onion, peeled and diced
1 green or red bell pepper, seeded and diced
Other options: celery, sliced cabbage, jalapeño peppers, bean sprouts, or any other leftover vegetables
3–4 cups cold cooked rice
2 eggs, whisked
2 tablespoons soy sauce

SERVES FOUR

- Heat the oil in a large skillet or cast-iron pan.
- Add the onion, peppers, and any other vegetables you like—do not add the bean sprouts at this stage, they should be tossed with the finished rice in order to maintain their crispness.
- Sauté the vegetables until the onion begins to brown.
- Add the cooked rice and stir-fry until the mixture begins to turn brown.
- Scramble the eggs in the rice pan. Push the rice away from the center of the pan and pour in the eggs. You may add a touch more oil if you like. (If there's no room in the pan, scramble the egg in a separate pan and mix it with the rice mixture at the end.)
- Once the egg is lightly cooked, toss all the ingredients together, add the soy sauce, and serve immediately.

PATIENCE

There's an old story about a hermit who puts a pot of rice over the fire, then sits down to meditate. He is disturbed by a knock at the door. His friends enter and he offers them supper, but the fire is just cold ash and, lifting off the pot's lid, they find the rice covered with mold—he'd been deep in meditation for weeks. This man wasn't a very good cook, but a damn good meditator. My experience is just the opposite. When I cook rice, it seems to take weeks to be ready. Does Zen practice make a person less impatient? If anything, I've become more aware of my inherently impatient nature.

GREEN BEANS WITH GINGER, CORN, AND MISO

Many Japanese dishes use a simple sauce made with miso, *a fermented soy and bean paste, available in most Asian or health food stores.*

Sometimes, the domestic miso available in health food stores is as good as the Japanese version and free from chemical additives and sugar. For this dish I recommend using a mild "white" miso.

INGREDIENTS

1 tablespoon peanut or vegetable oil
1 cup fresh raw corn kernels, removed from cob (see page 53)
1-inch piece of fresh ginger, peeled and minced
4 cups green beans, parboiled and chopped
½ cup sake or dry sherry
2 tablespoons white miso

SERVES FOUR

- Heat the oil in a skillet or a cast-iron pan. Add the corn kernels, minced ginger, and green beans.
- Sauté until the corn and beans are heated through.
- Add the sake and continue to cook until the liquid is reduced by half.
- Once reduced, stir in the miso.
- Then, remove from the heat and serve.

WATERMELON, BLUEBERRIES, AND MINT

These summer fruits taste delicious together and create a colorful and refreshing finale to this meal.

INGREDIENTS

4 cups watermelon, peeled, diced and seeded
2 cups blueberries
¼ lemon, juiced
A few sprigs of fresh mint, leaves removed from stem and torn into pieces

SERVES FOUR

- Place the watermelon and blueberries into a bowl and stir in the lemon juice and mint leaves.
- Serve cold.

FOCACCIA

Focaccia is a delicious Italian, yeasted flat bread, often topped with herbs, onions or roasted peppers. Sometimes the herbs are baked into the dough.

INGREDIENTS

1 ¼-ounce-packet active dry yeast
3½–4 cups all-purpose flour
5 tablespoons olive oil, plus extra for greasing
1 tablespoon salt
1 cup leftover mashed potatoes
½ cup fresh chopped sage

MAKES ONE LARGE LOAF

- Preheat oven to 400°F (200°C) and generously grease a 1-inch deep baking pan with oil.
- In a large bowl, activate the yeast in about 3½ cups of warm water for 5–10 minutes until a foamy layer forms on top of the water.
- Then, gradually add about 2 cups of flour to form a thick batter. Then allow the batter stand for about 45 minutes.
- Next, work in 3 tablespoons of the olive oil, the salt, mashed potatoes, and sage with a wooden spoon. Then, begin to add the rest of the flour.
- When the dough begins to come away from the sides of the bowl, turn it onto a well-floured surface and knead in the flour until the dough stops sticking to the surface. It should be shiny and elastic, and the perfectly distributed yeast will seem ready to stand up and burst into song. Soon it will all die in the oven, but for now…!
- Place the ball of dough in the greased pan and let it rest for about 10 minutes.
- The dough should now be elastic and pliable. Push it down into the shape of the flat pan, working it toward the edges. It should cover the whole pan. Leave for 30 minutes to double in size. If the dough has not doubled, let it sit longer—about another 30 minutes.
- Just before it goes in the oven, make indents in the surface of the dough with your fingers. This gives it the puckered surface usually associated with focaccia. You can also add toppings at this stage: roasted peppers work well, thinly sliced and distributed evenly over the surface of the dough, caramelized onions are also delicious.
- Spray the loaf with some olive oil and place it in the oven for 30 minutes until browned.
- Remove the focaccia from the oven and carefully take it out of the pan.
- Cut it into 3-inch squares and serve warm.

MINESTRONE SOUP

A mirepoix is a vegetable mixture that increases the flavor of this fine broth.

FOR THE MIREPOIX
1 tablespoon olive oil
1 onion, peeled and finely chopped
2 carrots, peeled and finely chopped
2 stalks celery, finely chopped
4 cloves garlic, peeled and finely chopped
1 small chili pepper, seeded
14-ounce can of whole tomatoes

FOR THE SOUP
½ cup white beans, soaked and drained
½ cup chickpeas, soaked and drained
1 sprig fresh rosemary
2 sprigs fresh thyme
Rind from a small piece of Parmesan cheese
2 carrots peeled and cut into chunks
4 red-skinned potatoes, peeled and chopped
½ cup green peas, fresh or frozen
1 zucchini, cut into chunks
1 handful of green beans, chopped

4 leaves of chard or kale, chopped
A few sprigs of fresh parsley, chopped
12 fresh basil leaves, torn
Salt and pepper to taste
Freshly grated Parmesan cheese to top
SERVES SIX TO EIGHT

- For the mirepoix, heat the oil in a skillet and sauté until the vegetables are soft. Add the garlic, chili pepper, and tomatoes and mash the mixture together.
- For the soup, place the mirepoix in a saucepan and add 12 cups of water, the white beans, and chickpeas. Bring to a boil then simmer for 1 hour until the beans begin to soften.
- Tie the rosemary, thyme, and the cheese rind in cheesecloth and add it to the soup with the carrots and potatoes. Simmer for a further 30 minutes.
- Add the rest of the vegetables and simmer for 10 minutes. Stir in the herbs, season to taste and top with the Parmesan cheese to serve.

ROASTED BEETS WITH BALSAMIC VINEGAR

INGREDIENTS
2 pounds beets, scrubbed
Balsamic vinegar to taste
Salt to taste
SERVES SIX

- Preheat oven to 400°F (200°C).
- Loosely wrap the washed beets in aluminum foil—large beets can be halved to speed up the cooking time. The foil should be tightly sealed with no gaps to ensure that the beets are thoroughly steamed.
- Place the beets in the preheated oven for 1 hour until fork-tender. Remove and set aside to cool.
- When the beets are cool enough to handle, peel them and cut into chunks.
- Toss with balsamic vinegar. Sprinkle with salt to taste and serve.

POTATO SALAD WITH ARUGULA AND OLIVES

I imagine that in eighty-five percent of the country, arugula is believed to be a lesser character from The Iliad, *but if you do have access to this unique bitter-tasting green, it is wonderful tossed in a salad or with pasta, and equally great in potato salad.*

INGREDIENTS

2 pounds potatoes, peeled and left whole
10 Kalamata olives, pitted and split in half
1 tablespoon capers
2 cups arugula, washed, dried and torn
1 lemon, juiced
1 shallot, peeled and minced
Salt and pepper to taste
2 tablespoons extra virgin olive oil

SERVES FOUR

- Boil the potatoes in a saucepan until fork tender and drain.
- When cool enough to handle, cut the potatoes into 1-inch cubes and spread them on a platter to cool further.
- When the potatoes are cooled, add the olives, capers, and arugula.
- In a separate bowl, mix the lemon juice, shallot, salt, and pepper, then whisk in the olive oil.
- Pour the mixture over the potatoes, toss lightly, and serve.

FRANK AND RITA'S

"Jesus is coming, look busy."
I saw this slogan on a tee-shirt. It sums up for me a certain aspect of what you might call a "Christian work ethic." It reminds me of my first restaurant job at a truck stop called "Frank and Rita's." I was applying for the job of dishwasher and was shown by Frank into a small, gray, windowless dishroom. There was no automatic dish washer; just a single sink piled high with the morning's dishes. It seemed that the previous dishwasher had vanished without notice. The room reeked of ancient grease and the walls, dripping and covered with stains, had a fleshy organic quality. It was as if I'd been led into the secret chamber of a diseased internal organ. My eyes desperately searched the small room for some ray of hope and fell on an old greasy sign which had been scotch-taped to the wall. "If you have time to lean, you have time to clean."

WHITE BEAN AND ROASTED GARLIC PUREE

This purée is great to have on hand; not only is it wonderful as a dip, but it also works well in lasagna. Roasted garlic keeps in the refrigerator for a few days.

INGREDIENTS
1 cup white beans, soaked overnight
1 bay leaf
1 head garlic
2 sprigs of fresh thyme, removed from the stem and minced
1 tablespoon lemon juice
3 tablespoons extra virgin olive oil, plus extra for spraying
Salt and pepper to taste
SERVES FOUR

- Preheat oven to 400°F (200°C).
- Place the beans in a saucepan. Cover them with water, leaving 2 inches of water above the level of the beans. Bring to the boil, then reduce the heat.
- Add the bay leaf and cook for at least 1 hour or until the beans are tender.
- Spray the garlic head with olive oil, and then wrap it loosely in aluminum foil. Place in the oven for 45 minutes. Check for softness; if the garlic is soft all the way through, it's ready. Remove and set aside to cool.
- When the garlic is cool enough to handle, slice off the top third and, using either your fingers or the blade of a knife, squeeze out the purée.
- When the beans are cooked, drain them, retaining the cooking water.
- Put the beans, the purée, the thyme, and lemon juice in a food processor.
- With the motor running, add the olive oil. If the purée is too thick for your liking, add a little of the reserved cooking water.
- Season with salt and pepper, and serve with slices of toasted country bread.

RALPH'S BEETS WITH MINT

INGREDIENTS
2 pounds beets, scrubbed
½ lemon, juiced
A handful of fresh mint leaves, torn
A pinch of salt
A few sprays of extra virgin olive oil
SERVES FOUR

- Preheat oven to 400°F (200°C).
- Wrap the beets in aluminum foil, sealed airtight, and bake for 1 hour until fork-tender. Remove from the oven and allow to cool.
- When cool enough to handle, peel and cut the the beets into large chunks.
- Meanwhile, place the lemon juice, mint, salt, and oil in a large bowl.
- Mix in the beets and serve.

TAMARIND POTATOES

The tartness of tamarind goes well with potatoes. This dish can be made ahead of time and reheated—just stir the potatoes and sauce together, cool and cover. It keeps in the refrigerator for up to 6 hours. To reheat, add a little water to the mixture, bring to a boil over a gentle heat and simmer for about 5 minutes to heat through.

INGREDIENTS

1 pound red potatoes, peeled and left whole
3 tablespoons butter or oil
1 teaspoon brown mustard seeds
1 medium onion, peeled and thinly sliced
2 jalapeño peppers, seeded and chopped
2 tablespoons tamarind pulp, seeds removed, softened in a little warm water
1 tablespoon sugar, preferably raw or brown
Salt to taste
½ cup chopped fresh cilantro leaves for garnish

SERVES FOUR

- Boil the potatoes in a large saucepan until fork-tender.
- Drain and set aside to cool. Once cool enough to handle, chop the potatoes into quarters and set aside.
- Heat the butter or oil in a large skillet.
- Add the mustard seeds and sauté until they begin to pop. Then add the onion to the skillet and sauté until browned.
- Now, add the chopped jalapeño, the tamarind, and the sugar.
- Simmer gently until the tamarind produces a thick sauce.
- Add the potatoes and continue to cook until the mixture is thoroughly heated. You may have to add a little water if the mixture seems too thick.
- Salt to taste and garnish with the cilantro leaves before serving.

TANTALIZING SMELLS

A chef I once worked with explained to me how various tastes and smells could be categorized by complexity. Roasting meat was absolutely off the top of the scale, while coffee rated a distant second. Third was chocolate. Not exactly the recipe for a healthy diet, but that's what we're up against: a collective memory reaching back into the dim recesses of time: "Meat and fire, the good life."

HERB AND GOAT CHEESE FRITTATA

Frittata *(the Italian word for omelet) is cooked in a heavy-based skillet without turning and then finished off under a preheated broiler. It is delicious eaten hot, lukewarm, or even cold.*

INGREDIENTS

6 eggs
1 bunch fresh sage or in combination with thyme, savory, dill, or parsley, chopped
Salt and pepper to taste
3 tablespoons butter or olive oil
1 shallot, peeled and chopped
10 cherry tomatoes, halved
4 ounces goat cheese, crumbled
Spray of olive oil

SERVES FOUR

- Preheat the broiler.
- In a bowl, beat together the eggs and fresh herbs. Season to taste with salt and pepper.
- Heat the butter or oil in a heavy-based skillet, add the shallot and sauté until just softened.
- Add the egg mixture, then cover and simmer for 10–15 minutes before removing the lid—the frittata should still be moist on top.
- Arrange the tomatoes and goat cheese over the surface, then spray lightly with olive oil and place under the broiler until well-browned.
- Remove from the skillet, cut the frittata into generous-sized wedges, and serve.

BANANA RAITA

Raita *is a refreshing Indian condiment traditionally made with plain yogurt and thinly sliced cucumber—here banana is used to create a unique fruity flavor ideal with the Tamarind Potatoes.*

INGREDIENTS

2 ripe bananas, peeled and sliced
1 cup plain yogurt
2 tablespoons chopped fresh mint
1 jalapeño pepper, seeded and finely chopped
½ teaspoon cumin seeds, toasted and ground

SERVES FOUR

- Put all the ingredients in a bowl and mix thoroughly.
- Cover and allow to stand for up to 2 hours before serving.

PASTA WITH SUMMER HERBS

Here is a dish where the usual considerations of measurement, and moderation for that matter, go out the window—you can't use too many fresh herbs in this preparation. The first step should be to plant an herb garden. This takes time, however, so it is more practical to find a grocery store that stocks fresh herbs and buy what looks best. Some possibilities are fresh thyme, oregano, summer savory, basil, lavender, Italian parsley, and cilantro.

The best part of this dish is sorting, cleaning, and chopping the various herbs as the indescribable aromas that result are fantastic. Of course, different combinations result in different flavors. Don't worry about amounts, just go easy on rosemary, summer savory, and oregano—their strong flavors may overpower your dish.

This is the most aromatic of preparations and you will notice that a good quality extra virgin olive oil will give off its own wonderful aroma as it's heated.

Usually, there's not much point in cooking with an expensive extra virgin olive oil because it burns easily, but for this dish the heat applied to the oil is minimal so it retains its fruity flavor.

INGREDIENTS

1 pound pasta, such as spaghetti, linguine or tagliatelle
Copious amounts of fresh green herbs
4 tablespoons extra virgin olive oil
1–2 cloves garlic, peeled and minced
Salt and pepper to taste
Shaving of Parmesan cheese to top

SERVES FOUR

- Cook the pasta until al dente (see recipe on page 117).
- Clean and chop all the herbs and set aside.
- Gently heat the olive oil in a skillet. Add the garlic and sauté over low heat until it just begins to brown. Then throw in all the herbs. It's amazing to see them rising to the surface of the oil like a fragrant green island. Cook the herbs for a couple of minutes only: don't overcook, the herbs should retain their intense green color.
- Remove from the heat, toss with the cooked pasta and garnish with a few shavings of Parmesan cheese to serve.

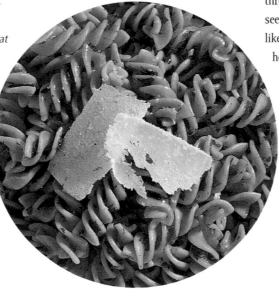

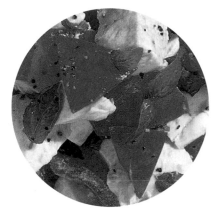

TOMATO, BASIL AND MOZZARELLA SALAD

This simple salad can double up as a wonderful, uncooked pasta sauce.

INGREDIENTS

4 large ripe tomatoes
12 ounces fresh mozzarella, cubed
1 cup fresh basil leaves, torn
½ cup extra virgin olive oil
Salt and pepper to taste

SERVES FOUR

- Cut the tomatoes in half, squeeze out and discard the juice and seeds, then cut the meat into chunks.
- Toss the mozzarella with the tomatoes, fresh basil, and olive oil in a bowl.
- Season to taste and serve.

Hanging Around

Everyone knows the usefulness of being useful, few know the usefulness of being useless.

Chuang Tzu

STRAWBERRIES WITH BALSAMIC VINEGAR

INGREDIENTS

Basket of fresh strawberries, washed and sliced, about 3 cups
2 tablespoons sugar
2 tablespoons balsamic vinegar

SERVES FOUR

- Place all the ingredients in a bowl and toss to combine.
- Cover the bowl with plastic wrap and allow the mixture to cool in the refrigerator for at least 1 hour.
- Serve cold.

Along the cedar-lined path of an old shrine
I gather leaves
As the sun sets.

Fall

QUINOA WITH PEARS
AND FETA CHEESE

Quinoa, like buckwheat, is not really a grain, but more of a nutritious weed—high in protein and quick to cook. It's best to prepare quinoa by slightly browning it in a heavy-based skillet, then cooking it like rice.

INGREDIENTS

1 cup quinoa
2 cups water
½ teaspoon salt
3 ripe pears, peeled, cored and chopped
¼ cup sliced almonds, lightly toasted
4 ounces feta cheese, crumbled
2 tablespoons olive oil
1 tablespoon fresh, snipped chives

SERVES FOUR

- Rinse the quinoa thoroughly in a fine mesh strainer and drain.
- Heat the quinoa in a heavy-based skillet, stirring constantly until the grains separate and begin to brown.
- Add the water and salt and bring to the boil, then reduce the heat and simmer for 15 minutes until all the liquid is absorbed.
- Transfer to a bowl and toss with the pears, almonds, and feta cheese.
- Drizzle with the olive oil and top with the fresh chives to serve.

70

BRUSSELS SPROUTS WITH ORANGE ZEST

INGREDIENTS

16 Brussels sprouts
2 tablespoons butter
1 shallot, peeled and minced
1 teaspoon orange zest
Optional: 2 teaspoons orange liqueur, such as Grand Marnier or Triple Sec
½ lime, juiced
Salt and pepper to taste

SERVES FOUR

- Remove the outer leaves from the Brussels sprouts and, using a paring knife, cut an "x" in the bottom of each—this helps the sprouts to cook evenly and quickly.
- Cook them in a saucepan of boiling salted water for about 8 minutes. Then drain and set aside to cool. Once cool enough to handle, cut in half.
- Meanwhile, melt the butter in a large skillet. Add the shallot and sauté until browned.
- Add the sprouts and continue to cook until fork-tender.
- Now add the orange zest and liqueur, if using, and sauté for 2–3 minutes.
- Remove from the heat and sprinkle with lime juice. Season with salt and pepper, and serve.

ROASTED ACORN SQUASH

Try to find small acorn squash—about the size of baseballs. Squash become sweeter the longer they are off the vine, so allow them to ripen.

INGREDIENTS

2 acorn squash, halved and seeded
2 tablespoons butter, softened
4 teaspoons brown sugar

SERVES FOUR

- Preheat oven to 375°F (190°C).
- Coat the inside of each squash half with ½ tablespoon of butter and 1 teaspoon of brown sugar.
- Place the squash, cut side up, in a baking dish and pour water around them to a height of about 1 inch.
- Bake in the oven for about 35 minutes, basting once with the butter and sugar.
- When the squash is fork-tender and browned on top, remove from the oven, and serve.

PENNE WITH TOMATO AND PAN-ROASTED VEGETABLE SAUCE

Here at the Zen Center, serving pasta in the meditation hall presents something of a challenge. Western Zen students are not so proficient at maneuvring chopsticks, so mostly everything is eaten with a spoon—leading to a dignified sort of shoveling. Penne lends itself well to this.

INGREDIENTS

1 pound penne pasta
1 red bell pepper
3 Japanese eggplants
1 large Portobello mushroom, or 2 cups domestic mushrooms, chopped
12 Roma tomatoes or a 14-ounce can of tomatoes
4 tablespoons olive oil
4 cloves garlic, peeled and finely chopped
5–6 fresh basil leaves, torn
Pepper to taste
Romano cheese, grated

SERVES FOUR

- Cook the penne until al dente (see recipe on page 117).
- If you are using a gas stove, turn the burner all the way up, and using tongs or a fork, hold the pepper directly in the flame. Turn it as the skin blackens.
- When the skin is evenly charred, though not burned through to the flesh, remove from the flame and allow to cool—the skin will easily scrape off. Don't worry about getting every black speck off—it is better to peel it rather than run the pepper under water to remove the skin, as that removes a lot of the flavor.
- Now, remove the seeds and slice the pepper into thin strips. Set aside.
- Chop the eggplants into 1-inch chunks. If Japanese eggplant or the miniature Indian variety is not available, a large eggplant cut into chunks will do fine.
- Place the eggplant in a colander and toss it with a handful of salt. Let it rest for about 1 hour to allow the salt to absorb the moisture and bitterness of the eggplant.
- Drain the eggplant on a paper towel, then pan-roast in a well-seasoned cast-iron skillet until browned. Then add the mushroom and continue to cook until the eggplant and mushroom are browned and tender. Remove from the heat and stir in the strips of red pepper. Set aside.
- Peel the tomatoes (see page 50). Remove and discard the seeds, then chop the meat. Set aside.
- Heat the oil in a saucepan and add the garlic. When the garlic begins to brown, throw in the chopped tomatoes.
- Cook over a low flame for about 20 minutes, stirring occasionally.
- Remove from the heat and purée in a blender or food processor.
- Return to the pan and then add the roasted vegetables.
- Add torn basil leaves, season with pepper, and toss with the hot pasta.
- Top with the grated Romano cheese and serve immediately.

ROASTED BEETS AND GREENS

The colors of this dish are beautiful deep reds and dark greens. The most flavorful way to cook a beet is to roast it in the oven as you would a potato.

INGREDIENTS
4–5 large beets with 8 cups greens
4 tablespoons olive oil
½ lemon, juiced
Salt and pepper
SERVES FOUR

- Preheat oven to 400°F (200°C).
- Remove the beet tops, wash them thoroughly and set aside.
- Wash the beets and wrap them loosely in aluminum foil. The foil should be airtight so that the beets can steam. Bake in the oven for 1 hour or until fork-tender.
- Remove from the oven and allow to cool. Once cool, peel them and cut them into generous chunks. Set aside.
- Cook the washed beet tops in a saucepan of boiling salted water for about 10 minutes, then drain and plunge into cold water. If you are unable to get beets with greens or the tops are not in good shape, any sort of greens will do: chard, spinach, or beet tops can be sautéed, but more hearty greens such as collard or mustard should be parboiled first.
- Drain and squeeze out as much water as you can, then chop the greens and set aside. Needless to say, greens cook down quite a bit, so at this point you can see whether you will have enough.
- Heat the oil in a cast-iron pan. Add the greens and sauté until softened.
- Add the cooked beets and the lemon juice to the pan and toss together until heated through.
- Season to taste and serve.

ARUGULA SALAD WITH SHAVED PARMESAN CHEESE

The wonderfully tangy bite of arugula and lemon complements the powerful flavors of the other dishes.

INGREDIENTS
1 or 2 bunches of arugula
1 lemon, juiced
2 teaspoons sea salt
½ cup olive oil
Shavings of Parmesan cheese
Freshly ground black pepper
SERVES FOUR

- Wash the arugula in a colander and dry on a paper towel. Arrange on a serving platter.
- Whisk together the lemon juice, sea salt, and olive oil in a bowl.
- Toss the dressing with the arugula and sprinkle it with shavings of Parmesan cheese.
- Add a generous amount of freshly ground pepper and serve.

PENNE WITH SWEET ONIONS AND ROASTED SQUASH

INGREDIENTS

1 small butternut squash, halved and seeded
3 large ripe tomatoes
1 large Vidalia or other sweet onion, peeled and cut into wedges
1 pound penne pasta
½ bunch fresh basil, leaves torn
2 tablespoons extra virgin olive oil
Salt and pepper
1¼ cups Parmesan cheese shavings

SERVES FOUR

- Preheat oven to 375°F (190°C).
- Place the butternut squash, cut side down, in a baking dish. Add ¼ cup of water and place in the oven for 50 minutes or until tender.
- Arrange the tomatoes and onion wedges on a separate baking dish or sheet pan and place in the oven for about 30 minutes or until the tomatoes and onions are soft.
- Cook the penne until al dente. (See page 117 for instructions on cooking pasta).

- Remove the squash, tomatoes, and onions from the oven. Skin the tomatoes, then roughly chop the flesh. Place in a bowl with the onion wedges.
- Spoon out the squash and mix it into the tomato and onion mixture along with the basil leaves, and olive oil.
- Season with salt and pepper, and toss with the hot penne.
- Top with Parmesan shavings to serve.

A Wonderful Secret

A little dab of salt and pickles
to help bring out the flavor,
a touch of ginger and cinnamon
to pick my spirits up.
On a clay stove, in a pot from Sheh
the poor family's salvation—
this wonderful secret
do I dare reveal it to the world?

Lu-Yu (1125–1210)

Translated by Burton Watson

BEET AND
BLOOD ORANGE SALAD

*When using citrus fruit in a salad, make
sure all the rind and pith is removed.*

INGREDIENTS

2 cups beets, cooked and chopped
½ red onion, peeled and thinly sliced
1–2 blood oranges, peeled, seeded, and chopped
1 tablespoon balsamic vinegar
2 teaspoons extra virgin olive oil
Salt and pepper to taste
Optional: orange zest to garnish
SERVES FOUR

- Toss together all ingredients in a large
  bowl. Season to taste and garnish with
  the orange zest.

GARLIC AND
LEMON RASAM

*Rasam is a spicy Indian soup usually
made with a base of dahl for stock
flavor. I usually use a red lentil, as they
are widely available and cook quickly.*

INGREDIENTS

¼ cup red lentils, rinsed
8 cups vegetable stock or water
1 tablespoon olive oil
3 small Japanese eggplants, chopped
4 cloves garlic, peeled and minced
2 jalapeño peppers, seeded and chopped
1 shallot, peeled and chopped
1 tomato, chopped
½ teaspoon turmeric
1 lemon, juiced
½ teaspoon peppercorns
½ teaspoon cumin seeds
SERVES FOUR

- In a large saucepan, bring the lentils
  and vegetable stock or water to the
  boil. Reduce the heat, partially cover,
  and simmer for 30 minutes, skimming
  off the cooking foam as it appears.
- Heat the oil in a heavy-based skillet.
  Add the eggplant, garlic, peppers, and
  shallot and sauté for 10 minutes.
- Then add the tomato, cooked lentils,
  turmeric, and lemon juice and simmer
  for a further 15 minutes.
- In a small spice grinder, crush the
  peppercorns and cumin seeds and add
  them to the soup.
- Season to taste and serve.

STEAMED COUSCOUS

Couscous is a North African cousin to pasta. It cooks fast and is available in most grocery stores. The couscous available in America is good, but is a far cry from the fantastically rich, fluffy, steamed couscous prepared in Moroccan households.

One way of cooking couscous is to stir it into boiling water, bring it back to a boil, then cover and remove it from the heat—it cooks very quickly. The following recipe uses the steaming method and comes very close to the authentic couscous of Morocco.

INGREDIENTS

1 cup couscous, rinsed
Spray of olive oil
2 tablespoons butter
½ teaspoon salt

SERVES FOUR

- Drape the top portion of a two-tiered steamer with cheesecloth. Spray the cloth with olive oil, then spread the rinsed couscous over the cloth, breaking up any clumps.
- Fill the lower pan with water and put the upper pan containing the couscous on top. Place it on the stovetop, cover and bring the water to a boil.
- Reduce the heat and steam the couscous for 20 minutes.
- Remove the couscous to a platter and spread it out with a spatula. Spray or sprinkle it with about ¼ cup of cold water. Then, return the couscous to the cheesecloth-lined pan and steam for a further 30 minutes.
- Transfer the couscous to a serving dish and toss it with the butter to coat the grains. Sprinkle with the salt and cover for 10 minutes before serving.

PAN-ROASTED GREEN BEAN SALAD WITH PINE NUTS, MINT AND FETA

INGREDIENTS

1 pound green beans, cleaned
10 Kalamata olives, pitted and chopped
¼ cup pine nuts, toasted
1 tablespoon extra virgin olive oil
½ lemon, juiced
½ cup feta cheese, crumbled
¼ cup fresh mint, chopped
Freshly ground black pepper to taste

SERVES FOUR

- Parboil the green beans in a saucepan until just tender, then plunge into ice water. Drain.
- Heat a cast-iron pan and add the beans. Cook until they are dry and begin to blacken around the edges.
- Remove from the heat and transfer to a bowl. Add the olives, pine nuts, olive oil, lemon juice, feta cheese, and mint. Toss together gently.
- Season well with freshly ground black pepper and serve.

VEGETABLE TAGINE

Tagine *is the earthenware pot used to prepare this traditional Moroccan meat stew. The first time I had it was after I had spent three weeks crossing the Sahara, living mostly on oranges and flat bread. It was in a restaurant in Casablanca and the tagine came to the table in a huge earthenware tureen—it tasted incredible.*

Here I have created a vegetarian version. If possible, use an earthenware pot, as the flavor will greatly benefit. Start the recipe on the stove and finish it in a hot oven for one hour.

INGREDIENTS

2 tablespoons butter or oil
1 onion, peeled and chopped
2 cloves garlic, peeled and chopped
½ cup red lentils, rinsed
5 plum tomatoes, chopped, or a 14-ounce can of whole tomatoes
4 carrots, peeled and roughly chopped
1 stalk celery, chopped
Vegetable stock or water to cover the ingredients
1 teaspoon turmeric
1 teaspoon cinnamon
½ cup raisins
½ pound new potatoes, halved or quartered
1-inch piece of fresh ginger, peeled
1–2 jalapeño peppers, seeded
½ cup cilantro or parsley
¼ teaspoon lemon zest
Salt and pepper to taste

SERVES FOUR

- Heat the butter or oil in a heavy-based steel or earthenware pot.
- Add the onion and garlic, and sauté until lightly browned.
- Add the rinsed lentils, tomatoes, carrots, and celery. Then add the stock or water to cover and bring to a boil.
- Add the turmeric, cinnamon, and raisins and simmer for 30 minutes.
- Now add the potatoes and continue cooking for 12–15 minutes or until fork-tender.
- Meanwhile, place the ginger, peppers, cilantro or parsley, and lemon zest in a food processor and purée. Add to the pot and allow to simmer for a few more minutes.
- Season with salt and pepper to taste and serve.

STUFFED GREEN PEPPERS
WITH SALSA

The southwestern-style stuffing is given extra spice by the inclusion of rich, red salsa. Any kind of bell pepper will do for stuffing, but green are readily available and contrast well with salsa.

FOR THE SALSA

2 large tomatoes seeded, peeled and chopped
1 small onion, peeled and diced
1 clove garlic, peeled and crushed
2 jalapeño peppers, seeded and chopped
2 tablespoons fresh chopped cilantro
Lime juice
Salt and pepper to taste
Optional: crushed red pepper for a hotter salsa

FOR THE PEPPERS

1½ cups cooked white rice
¼ cup currants or white raisins
¼ cup pine nuts, toasted
4 ounces goat cheese
Salt and pepper to taste
4 green bell peppers
SERVES FOUR

- Preheat oven to 350°F (180°C).
- To make the salsa, mix together all the ingredients in a small bowl, adding the lime juice and seasoning to your taste. Set aside.
- To prepare the pepper stuffing, mix together the rice, currants, pine nuts, and ½ cup of salsa. Pour into a food processor. Add the goat cheese and seasoning and combine with a few short bursts—the mixture should not be smooth.
- Slice the tops off the green peppers and remove the seeds. Fill the peppers with the stuffing mixture and replace the tops.
- Place the peppers in a shallow baking pan and bake in the oven for 45 minutes.
- Remove from the oven, top with the remaining salsa and serve.

You'll Really Think it's Funny

Everyone eats rice yet no one knows why. When I say this now people laugh at me, but instead of laughing along with them you should step back and give it some thought. Think it over and I guarantee the time will come when you'll really think it's funny.

Ryokan

ROASTED FENNEL WITH OLIVES, ROSEMARY AND THYME

Roasting fennel mutes its licorice-like flavor and softens its crunchy texture. Tossing the fennel in balsamic vinegar before roasting, as I have done here, gives it an extra subtle and delicate flavor with a tart edge. The addition of olives and pungent herbs creates a wonderfully tasty vegetable side dish.

INGREDIENTS

2 large bulbs fennel, halved and thinly sliced
10 Kalamata olives
Dash of balsamic vinegar
1 tablespoon olive oil, plus extra for greasing
1 teaspoon fresh minced thyme
½ teaspoon fresh minced rosemary
Salt and pepper to taste

SERVES FOUR

- Preheat oven to 400°F (200°C). Lightly grease a baking sheet with some oil.
- Place all ingredients in a large bowl and mix together.
- Spread them out evenly onto the baking sheet and roast in the oven for 15–20 minutes until the fennel is browned at the edges.
- Serve immediately.

PAN-ROASTED APPLES WITH CINNAMON

INGREDIENTS

2 tablespoons butter
2 pounds apples, peeled, cored and quartered
1 tablespoon sugar
1 teaspoon cinnamon

SERVES FOUR

- Melt the butter in a skillet. Add the apples and sprinkle them with the sugar. Cook until the apples begin to caramelize.
- Then, reduce the heat and stir the apples gently. Continue cooking until thoroughly softened.
- Remove from the skillet, sprinkle with cinnamon, and serve.

HERB-ENCRUSTED POTATOES

This is one of my favorite dishes. It is simple to prepare, and the variety of fresh herbs can vary depending on what's available—I think rosemary is the best, but parsley and green onion are also delicious, or try all three chopped up together.

People often tell me that when they try to duplicate this recipe at home, it never works. It always warms a cook's heart to hear that. The truth is that the success of this and many of the dishes in this book depends on how effectively you can get your particular oven to perform. What's called for in this recipe is a lot of heat. Ideally, the heat should come from the bottom of the oven; don't set the pan on the heating element itself. If you are using an electric oven, get the pan as close to the source of the heat as you can.

INGREDIENTS

Spray of olive oil
Variety of fresh herbs, finely chopped
Salt and pepper
2 pounds new potatoes, halved or quartered, depending on size

SERVES FOUR

- Preheat oven to 450°F (230°C).
- Spray a sheet pan with a generous coating of olive oil.
- Sprinkle a handful of chopped fresh herbs over the surface of the oiled pan—you really can't use too much!
- Then, sprinkle salt and pepper over the herbs and arrange the potatoes with a cut side down on top of the herbs.
- Place in the oven for about 40 minutes. The potatoes should be tender and golden brown, and the cooked herbs should form a flavorful crust.

WHITE BEAN PROVENCALE

The vegetables and beans produce such a flavorsome stock that it's hard to believe this isn't a meat cassoulet.

INGREDIENTS

½ pound small white beans, soaked overnight
1 bay leaf
2 tablespoons olive oil
1 onion, peeled and chopped
2 cloves garlic, peeled and minced
1 carrot, peeled and chopped
1 pound fresh tomatoes, chopped or a 14-ounce can tomatoes
2 sprigs fresh thyme or a pinch dried thyme
5–10 leaves of fresh basil
Salt and pepper to taste

SERVES FOUR

- Drain the soaked beans, then cook in a saucepan with 3 pints of water and a bay leaf. Simmer for about 1½ hours until the beans begin to soften. Once cooked, drain the beans and reserve the cooking water. Set aside.

ASPARAGUS WITH LEMON
AND CAPERS

- Meanwhile, heat the olive oil in a heavy-based pot, large enough to hold the cooked beans and add the onion, garlic, and carrot and sauté for 2–3 minutes.
- Add the chopped tomato (drain the canned tomato, but reserve the liquid) and stir.
- Then add the beans to the pot and sauté for a further 2–3 minutes.
- Stir in the cooking water from the beans and, if you are using the canned tomatoes, the juice. Then throw in the fresh or dried thyme.
- Continue simmering the mixture for about 15–20 minutes or until the beans are very tender. The amount of liquid needed will depend on how long it takes the beans to finish cooking.
- The flavor intensifies as the beans finish cooking, so taste as you go along and add hot water if needed.
- When the beans are ready, stir in the fresh basil leaves.
- Season to taste and serve.

Refreshing the asparagus in cold water helps to retain its characteristic bright-green color. This clean-tasting dish is also good with the addition of a chopped boiled egg which makes it more substantial.

INGREDIENTS

1 large bunch asparagus
1 lemon, juiced
8 tablespoons olive oil
1 teaspoon salt
1 tablespoon capers
Freshly ground black pepper

SERVES FOUR

- Remove and discard the fibrous ends of the asparagus. Then, cook the asparagus in a large pot of boiling salted water for 6–8 minutes.
- Just as the asparagus begins to turn a brighter green, remove from the hot water and immediately run under cold water.

- Drain the asparagus and arrange on a serving platter.
- Now, pour the lemon juice into a small bowl and whisk in the olive oil and then the salt.
- Add the capers, then pour the dressing over the cooked and cooled asparagus.
- Season with freshly ground pepper and serve.

ESCAROLE WITH GORGONZOLA AND RED ONIONS

INGREDIENTS

2 tablespoons balsamic vinegar
2 teaspoons chopped fresh thyme
1 teaspoon salt
1 teaspoon freshly ground black pepper
2 pounds Gorgonzola cheese, crumbled
3–4 tablespoons olive oil
1 head escarole, washed and dried
1 red onion, peeled and sliced into thin half rings

SERVES FOUR

Eat

*Someone asked Master Yun Men,
"What is the most urgent phrase?"
The Master said, "Eat."*

Anonymous

- In a small bowl, mix together the balsamic vinegar, thyme, salt, pepper, and Gorgonzola cheese.
- Slowly whisk in the olive oil until well blended, thickened, and to your taste.
- Tear the escarole using your hands and arrange it with the red onion rings on a serving platter.
- Toss the escarole and onion with the dressing and serve.

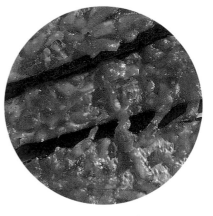

BAKED ZUCCHINI

INGREDIENTS

4–6 small zucchini, washed and halved lengthwise
1 tablespoon olive oil
3 cloves garlic, peeled and minced
Salt and pepper to taste
3 tablespoons Parmesan cheese

SERVES FOUR

- Preheat oven to 400°F (200°C).
- Arrange the zucchini, cut side up, in a baking dish.
- Brush or spray the cut side with the olive oil, then sprinkle with the garlic, salt and pepper, and Parmesan cheese.
- Place in the hot oven for 15 minutes until the cheese is browned.
- Serve immediately.

VEGETABLE PAELLA

This is a vegetarian version of the traditional Spanish dish paella, which usually contains seafood and chicken. The meat and fish create a flavorsome stock in the traditional dish, but if you are making a vegetarian version, a good vegetable stock, seasoned well with saffron will be equally tasty. I usually use a Dutch oven instead of a paella pan to make this dish, but any pot or pan that can withstand a lot of heat and has a tight-fitting lid will do.

INGREDIENTS

4 cups vegetable stock
1–2 pinches saffron
3 tablespoons olive oil
1 small onion, peeled and diced
1–2 cloves garlic, peeled and minced
2 carrots, peeled and diced
1 small green bell pepper, seeded and diced
2 cups short-grain white rice
Salt and pepper to taste
1 tablespoon sherry
1 pound fresh peas
½ cup chopped fresh parsley for garnish

SERVES FOUR

- Preheat oven to 475°F (240°C).
- Warm the stock in a large saucepan and add the saffron.
- Heat the olive oil in a Dutch oven or paella pan. Add the onion and sauté for a 2–3 minutes. Add the garlic, carrots, and green pepper and continue to sauté for a further 3–4 minutes or until the vegetables begin to soften.
- Now, add the rice, stirring well to coat the grains in the oil and vegetables.
- Season with salt and pepper and then add the sherry, warmed stock, and fresh peas.
- Bring the liquid almost to a boil, then cover, and place the pan in the oven for about 30 minutes until all the stock has been absorbed by the rice.
- Garnish with the parsley and serve.

POLENTA LASAGNA WITH MUSHROOM RAGU

Mushroom Ragu will satisfy cravings for hearty cold-weather fare in the waning daylight of fall. The mushroom ragu keeps for a few days in the refrigerator and is great with pasta. Here it's used as the sauce in a tasty lasagna.

INGREDIENTS

Olive oil for greasing

3½ cups water

1 cup coarse ground polenta (cornmeal)

2 teaspoons salt

1–2 ounces dried mushrooms (porcini, shiitake or morels)

1 tablespoon olive oil

2 shallots, peeled and diced

4 cloves garlic, peeled and diced

¼ pound mushrooms, sliced

1 large Portobello mushroom, sliced

½ teaspoon chopped fresh rosemary

1 teaspoon fresh thyme

2 cups dry white or red wine

12 ounces fontina cheese

Salt and pepper to taste

SERVES FOUR

- Preheat oven to 350°F (180°C). Spray a shallow baking pan with the olive oil and grease a large baking dish.
- To prepare the polenta, bring the water to a boil in a large saucepan. Whisk in the polenta and salt and continue stirring until it returns to the boil.
- Reduce the heat and simmer, stirring constantly, for 20 minutes until cooked. Have a kettle of hot water to hand, so you can thin the cereal if it begins to get too thick before reaching a smooth consistency. It should not be grainy and you should end up with a mixture with the consistency of porridge that a wooden spoon will stand up in.
- Pour the polenta into the baking pan and set aside to cool.
- To prepare the mushroom ragu, place the dried mushrooms in a bowl and pour over boiling water. Cover and leave it to steep for about 20 minutes.
- Heat the olive oil in a heavy-based skillet, add the shallots, garlic, and domestic and Portobello mushrooms and sauté until the mushrooms are browned.
- Drain the dried mushrooms and retain the liquid. Chop them and add them to the skillet. If the reconstituted mushrooms seem gritty, run them under the tap before chopping.
- Continue to sauté the mushrooms until they release water and soften. Then, add the herbs and wine and bring to a boil.
- Reduce the heat and simmer uncovered for about 45 minutes, adding the reserved mushroom soaking water when needed—if you run out, add water or vegetable stock. You should end up with a thick, intensely flavored sauce. Season to taste.
- Slice the cooled polenta into 2-inch squares. Then, line the oiled baking dish with layers of polenta, then mushroom ragu, then sliced fontina cheese. Build up about 2–3 layers, ending with the cheese.
- Place in the oven for 10 minutes, then serve or set aside to re-heat later.

GREEN BEANS WITH WAKAME

Wakame *is seaweed similar to kelp. After being soaked for a few minutes it can be sliced thinly and either eaten raw or sautéed in olive oil.*

INGREDIENTS

1 pound green beans, cleaned, cut and parboiled.
1 tablespoon olive oil
2 pounds wakame, soaked and thinly sliced
1 teaspoon soy sauce or shoyu
½ tablespoon toasted sesame seeds

SERVES FOUR

- Plunge the parboiled beans into ice water to retain their color.
- Heat a heavy-based skillet, then add beans. Sauté for 2–3 minutes or until the beans have dried off, then add the olive oil and wakame.
- Sauté for a further 2–3 minutes, then stir in the soy sauce.
- Remove the skillet from the heat and transfer the beans and wakame to a serving plate.
- Garnish with the toasted sesame seeds and serve immediately.

Not Myself

One day after the noon meal I came upon the Tenzo Yong drying some mushrooms in the sun. He had a bamboo stick in his hand and no hat on his head. The sun was scorching the pavement. His backbone was bent like a bow, and his eyebrows were white as a crane. I asked the poor fellow, "How long have you been a monk?" "Sixty-eight years," he replied. "It's too hot," I said, "Why don't you let your assistant do this?" He continued working, pausing only to reply, "Others are not myself."

Dogen

SWEET SAKE CARROTS

Many Japanese dishes make use of the contrasting flavors of sake, sugar, and soy sauce. As in the previous dish, the vegetables are parboiled, then sautéed.

INGREDIENTS

5 large carrots, cut into chunks
½ tablespoon vegetable oil
2 teaspoons sugar
2 tablespoons sake
Soy sauce to taste

SERVES FOUR

- Parboil the carrots in a saucepan for about 5 minutes. Drain, cool, and then dry them carrots on a paper towel.
- Now, heat the oil in a heavy-based skillet and add the carrots.
- Sauté them for 2–3 minutes, then add the sugar and sake.
- Continue cooking until most of the liquid has reduced.
- Season with soy sauce and serve.

VEGETABLE TEMPURA

Vegetable tempura is a variety of seasonal vegetables that are quickly deep-fried in the simplest of batters and taken to your table still sizzling hot.

Trying to get similar results at home is tricky. There are three important factors: cold batter, hot oil, and a light, low-gluten flour—cake flour is probably the best choice.

Most vegetables work well but my favorites are sliced Portobello mushrooms; peeled and thinly sliced sweet potato; large rings of peeled and sliced sweet onion; asparagus with the ends removed; green beans; whole scallions; and large slices of pepper.

INGREDIENTS

3–4 cups peanut or vegetable oil
2 cups cake flour
2 cups ice water
1 raw egg yolk
An array of sliced vegetables, washed and dried

SERVES FOUR

- Heat 3 inches of oil in a heavy-based pan over medium-high heat.
- Lightly whisk together the flour, ice water, and egg yolk in a bowl. The batter should remain lumpy as this makes the tempura lighter.
- Dip the vegetable pieces into the batter in batches and then drop them immediately into the hot oil.
- Fry the vegetables for 1–2 minutes on each side, then remove from the pan and allow them to drain on a paper towel.
- Dip and fry the remaining vegetables. Serve immediately with the Tempura Dipping Sauce (see right).

TEMPURA DIPPING SAUCE

- Mix together equal amounts of sake, soy sauce, sugar, and water.
- Garnish with thinly sliced scallions.

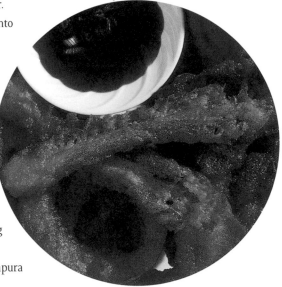

FRIED TOFU

Cornstarch makes an interesting batter for frying tofu. For best results, use firm or extra-firm tofu and serve the dish immediately after frying—the crispy batter quickly turns gummy. Serve with Tempura Dipping Sauce.

INGREDIENTS

3–4 cups peanut oil for frying
2 tablespoons cornstarch
2 tablespoons water
9-ounce package firm tofu, drained, dried, and cut into 1-inch cubes
2 scallions for garnish

SERVES FOUR

- Heat the peanut oil in a large pan, about 1-inch deep.
- Whisk together the cornstarch and the water in a bowl to form a batter.
- Dip the tofu cubes into the batter, then fry in the hot oil for 3–4 minutes until browned on both sides.
- When they are brown all over, remove the cubes from the oil and allow them to drain on a paper towel.
- Garnish with the scallions and serve.

TROPICAL FRUIT SALAD WITH COCONUT

INGREDIENTS

1 papaya, peeled, seeded, and chopped into chunks
2 mangoes, peeled, seeded, and chopped
1 pineapple, peeled, cored, and chopped
½ teaspoon cardamom powder
14-ounce can coconut milk
½ cup honey
Zest of one lime, thinly sliced

SERVES FOUR

- Place all the fruit in a bowl and gently mix in the cardamom. Then add the coconut milk and honey.
- Sprinkle the lime zest over the fruit mixture and serve.

RIGATONI WITH SLOW-ROASTED TOMATO SAUCE

Slow-roasted Tomatoes (see recipe on page 93) are an ideal base for a quick, easy and intensely flavored pasta sauce. Here, I have added some fresh basil to create an authentic Mediterranean taste.

INGREDIENTS

1 pound rigatoni
1 batch Slow-roasted Tomatoes
1 cup fresh basil leaves, rinsed
2 tablespoons olive oil
Shavings of Parmesan cheese

SERVES FOUR

- Cook the pasta until al dente (see instructions on page 117).
- Meanwhile, place the slow-roasted tomatoes in a food processor with the rinsed fresh basil leaves.
- Roughly purée with a few short bursts. With the motor running, gradually add the olive oil.
- Toss the tomato sauce with the hot rigatoni and serve with shavings of Parmesan cheese.

Mystical herb

A monk asked, "What about it when the mystical herb has not yet sprouted?"
The Master said, "If their fragrance is smelled your brains will fall out."

Record of Chou-Chou

Translated by James Green

FRENCH LENTILS WITH GOAT CHEESE, OLIVES, AND FRESH THYME

INGREDIENTS

1½ cups French lentils
5 cups water
1 bay leaf
1 carrot, peeled and diced
1 shallot or small onion, peeled and diced
2 sprigs fresh thyme
1 cup green olives, pitted and chopped
3 ounces goat cheese, crumbled
2 tablespoons extra virgin olive oil
Salt and pepper to taste

SERVES FOUR

- Rinse the lentils thoroughly in a colander, then place them in a saucepan with the water.
- Bring to a boil, then add the bay leaf, carrot, shallot or onion, and thyme sprigs. Simmer for about 30 minutes until the lentils are tender.
- Drain and transfer to a serving bowl. Add the olives, goat cheese, and extra virgin olive oil and stir well to mix all the ingredients.
- Season to taste with salt and pepper and serve immediately.

WARM ESCAROLE SALAD WITH LEMON GARLIC DRESSING

INGREDIENTS

2 cloves garlic, peeled and crushed
1 teaspoon salt
1 small lemon, juiced
About 2 tablespoons extra virgin olive oil
1 large head escarole, washed and chopped
Fresh ground pepper

SERVES FOUR

- In a small wooden bowl, mix the crushed garlic, salt, and lemon juice.
- Whisk in enough olive oil to form a thick emulsion.
- Heat a cast-iron pan and add the washed, chopped escarole. Toss while cooking until it begins to wilt.
- Remove from the heat and transfer to a serving platter.
- Drizzle with the dressing and serve.

Wind and snow, then snow and rain:
tonight, awakened by the cry of a wild goose
In the dark, endless winter sky.

Winter

LINGUINE WITH GARLIC, RAPINI AND BREAD CRUMBS

Rapini, also called broccoli rabe, has a dramatic flavor—bracing and mustardy. It goes very well with garlic. Here, tossed with linguine and bread crumbs, it makes a hearty dish.

INGREDIENTS

1 pound rapini
1 pound linguine
3 tablespoons olive oil
3 cloves garlic, peeled and chopped
3 tablespoons bread crumbs
Shavings of Parmesan cheese
Salt and pepper to taste

SERVES FOUR

- Rinse the rapini, remove the stems and cut the greens into 1-inch pieces.
- Place in a saucepan and parboil in salted water for about 5 minutes.
- Remove the rapini, reserving the cooking water, and immediately plunge it into cold water, then put the rapini in a colander and set aside.
- Next, cook the linguine in the reserved rapini water until al dente (see instructions on page 117). You may need to add more water.
- Meanwhile, heat the olive oil in a large skillet. Add the garlic and sauté until it begins to brown. Now throw in the parboiled rapini.
- Sauté for a further 2–3 minutes, then add the bread crumbs.
- Remove the skillet from the heat and toss with the cooked linguine in a large serving bowl.
- Top with shavings of Parmesan cheese, season to taste, and serve.

KITCHEN TIPS

"Looking busy" is a practice that restaurant workers quickly become proficient at. Here are my favorite tips:

1. Refrigeration Contemplation
Open and stare into the refrigerator as if contemplating the void. The expression on your face should be one of intense questioning. Continue until your supervisor has left the room.

2. The Aborted Journey
Set off from one side of the kitchen to the other. At midpoint, stop dead in your tracks with a thoughtful expression on your face; breathe deeply. Appearing annoyed or slightly confused, turn on your heels and head back the way you came. Repeat indefinitely.

3. Polish Whatever is at Hand
Always carry a rag so that at the slightest provocation you can shift into diligent polishing mode.

SLOW-ROASTED TOMATOES

These wonderful and intensely flavored tomatoes are great to have on hand. They can be chopped and tossed with hot pasta or served as delicious bite-sized appetizers. The only drawback is that they take a long time to roast, but they only need scant preparation time. You can either roast the tomatoes as instructed in this recipe or place them in a preheated oven, set to about 100°F (35°C), overnight.

INGREDIENTS
20 plum tomatoes
2 tablespoons olive oil
1 small onion, peeled and minced
3 cloves garlic, peeled and minced
½ teaspoon sugar
½ teaspoon red pepper flakes
Chopped fresh basil, thyme or rosemary
Salt and pepper to taste
SERVES FOUR

- Preheat oven to 200°F (100°C). Cover a large baking pan with wax paper.
- Slice the plum tomatoes in half and arrange on the covered baking pan.
- Heat 1 tablespoon of the olive oil in a small skillet.
- Add the minced onion and garlic and sauté until softened but not browned.
- Now add the sugar, red pepper flakes, and herbs, stir briefly, then remove from the heat.
- Spoon a small amount of the onion and garlic mixture onto each tomato and drizzle with the remaining oil.
- Season with salt and pepper and place in the preheated oven for 3 hours.
- Serve warm or at room temperature.

CARROT AND PARSNIP PUREE WITH FRESH TARRAGON

This root vegetable purée has a creamy texture and a delicious, aromatic flavor.

INGREDIENTS
5 large carrots, peeled and chopped
2 large parsnips, peeled and chopped
1 Idaho potato, peeled and chopped
1 tablespoon olive oil or butter
½ cup milk, cream, vegetable stock or water
2 teaspoons fresh tarragon
Salt and pepper to taste
SERVES FOUR

- Place the vegetables into a saucepan of rapidly boiling water and cook for 5–6 minutes or until tender.
- Drain, and if *not* using cream or stock, reserve the cooking water.
- Purée the vegetables and the oil or butter in a food processor. With the motor running, slowly add the milk or cream. For a low-fat version, use the reserved vegetable stock or water.
- Remove to a bowl and whisk in the tarragon, salt, and pepper and serve.

BRAISED FENNEL WITH PEAR AND STILTON CHEESE

This is a hearty dish that combines the gentle flavor of crunchy fennel, the sharpness and tanginess of Stilton, and the sweetness of juicy pears.

INGREDIENTS

2 tablespoons butter or olive oil
2 large bulbs fennel, thinly sliced
1 ripe pear, peeled and sliced
¼ cup Stilton cheese, crumbled

SERVES FOUR

- Heat the butter or oil in a skillet or braising pan.
- Add the fennel and toss to coat with butter or oil. Sauté for a couple of minutes only.
- Reduce the heat, cover, and braise for 20 minutes, tossing the fennel once or twice, until the fennel is well browned.
- Add the pear slices and toss with the fennel. Then remove from the heat.
- Transfer the fennel and pear mixture to a serving dish and top with the crumbled Stilton.

MASHED AND BROWNED RED-SKINNED POTATOES WITH GARLIC

INGREDIENTS

1 pound small red-skinned potatoes, washed, and halved
3 tablespoons olive oil
3 cloves garlic, peeled, and minced
Salt and pepper to taste
1 tablespoon snipped fresh chives

SERVES FOUR

- Cook the potatoes in a saucepan of boiling water for 15–20 minutes until fork-tender. Drain, return them to the pan, and cover. Set aside.
- Heat the oil in a cast-iron skillet until hot. Then remove from the heat and add the garlic and potatoes.

TWINING VINES

There are expectations, beliefs, and innumerable conditions all coming together making a meal. When we sit down to a wonderful meal, we encounter innumerable strands of phenomena. As Dogen says, "twining vines."

BAKED APPLE WITH WALNUTS, PRUNES, AND CINNAMON

INGREDIENTS
4 large Golden Delicious apples
Dash of lemon juice
½ cup walnuts
8 pitted prunes, chopped
1 tablespoon brown sugar
2 tablespoons cold butter
¼ teaspoon cinnamon
SERVES FOUR

- Preheat oven to 350°F (180°C).
- Carefully cut a 1-inch cap from the top of each apple, and set aside. Using a small spoon, remove the core and a small amount of flesh from each apple.

- Sprinkle a little lemon juice over the cut sections of each apple to stop them going brown.
- Put the walnuts, chopped prunes, sugar, butter, and cinnamon in a food processor and combine with a few short bursts. The mixture should be lumpy, not puréed.
- Fill each apple cavity with the mixture and replace the caps. Arrange the apples in a shallow baking dish and bake in the oven for 30 minutes.
- Once cooked, carefully remove the apples from the baking dish, transfer to serving plates, and serve piping hot.

- Using a potato masher, gently crush the potatoes into the hot oil and garlic.
- Return to the skillet to the heat and cook over a low heat until the potatoes are browned.
- Season with salt and pepper to taste.
- Scrape the mixture from the bottom of the skillet using a metal spatula and transfer it to a serving plate.
- Garnish the potatoes with the snipped chives and serve.

CARROTS WITH HIZIKI

Hiziki *is a sea vegetable available in most health food or Japanese markets. This dish works well if cooked in a heavy-based pan with a lid. Most Japanese "country style" cooks use cast-iron pans for this dish. I usually start by browning the carrots and onions in a heavy-based cast-iron pan without oil—this makes the carrots taste very sweet.*

INGREDIENTS

1 ounce hiziki soaked for 30 minutes in 3 cups of cold water
3 large carrots, peeled and cut into matchsticks
1 tablespoon vegetable oil
1 red onion, peeled and thinly sliced
1 teaspoon sugar
Pinch of cayenne
Soy sauce to taste
Handful of toasted sunflower seeds for garnish

SERVES FOUR

- Drain the hiziki, retaining the soaking water. Squeeze the excess water from the hiziki with your hands or blot with a paper towel—dry hiziki sautés more effectively. Set aside.
- Place the carrots in a heavy-based pan and sauté them until the edges begin to blacken.
- Now, pour in the oil and the onion. Be careful that the pan isn't so hot that the oil burns. Sauté until the onion begins to soften. If you don't have a cast-iron pan, heat the oil first before adding the carrots and onion.
- Add the drained hiziki and sauté for a further 2–3 minutes, then add the sugar, cayenne, and enough of the reserved hiziki soaking liquid to cover.
- Reduce the heat, cover the pan, and simmer for 15 minutes.
- Remove the lid and allow the liquid to reduce to the thickness of your taste.
- Taste for seasoning, adding soy sauce if necessary. Garnish with toasted sunflower seeds and serve.

KIM CHEE

Kim chee *is a garlicky, hot pickled cabbage that people either love or hate. But, it's great with beer. You can buy it in Korean markets or try making a less-pickled, fresher tasting version yourself—this recipe does not require any special pickle-making equipment and it makes enough for about eight servings. You can keep kim chee in the refrigerator for three days, but ensure it is totally covered as it may smell.*

INGREDIENTS

1 pound Napa cabbage, finely chopped and stalks discarded
2 teaspoons sea salt
4 cloves garlic, peeled and minced
1-inch piece of ginger, peeled and thinly sliced
¼–½ teaspoon cayenne pepper
5 scallions, cut into 1-inch pieces

MAKES ABOUT TWO CUPS

SOBA NOODLES WITH
GARLIC AND MUSHROOMS

- Toss all ingredients together in a crock or ceramic bowl until they are thoroughly mixed.
- Cover with a plate, small enough to fit inside the crock or bowl, then weight the plate down (cans of food will do) so it begins to squeeze the excess water out of the cabbage. Allow the mixture to sit for 4–5 hours. If you have a special pickle crock, you can let it sit for up to three days as the taste will greatly benefit.

When the Japanese cook noodles, they bring them to an initial boil, then add a cup of cold water—it's called surprise water and it reduces the heat in the pot. Then the water is brought back to the boil and the action repeated.

This dish may not come out perfectly the first time, but don't worry. At the point of serving, you may find that the dish has turned into a glutinous blob. If so, or if the noodles fall apart, they may be overcooked.

INGREDIENTS

1 pound soba or udon noodles
2 tablespoons peanut or vegetable oil
3 cloves garlic, peeled and chopped
3 cups domestic mushrooms, sliced
2 tablespoons sake or sherry
A handful of chopped scallions for garnish
Soy sauce to taste

SERVES FOUR

- Bring about 8 pints of water to a rolling boil. Add the noodles and cook for about 10 minutes until softened. Stir often to stop the noodles from sticking together.
- When the noodles are firm to the bite, al dente, turn off the heat, cover the pot, and let it sit for 2–3 minutes.
- Then, pour the noodles into a colander and run them under cold water until completely cooled. Drain and set aside.
- Meanwhile, heat the oil in a large cast-iron pan and add the garlic. Sauté until it begins to brown, then add the mushrooms. Sauté these until they are soft and browned.
- Add the sake, then the noodles and cook until they are heated through.
- Divide onto four serving plates and garnish with the scallions. Season with soy sauce to taste and serve immediately.

WINTER SQUASH SOUP

The taste of squash improves as it ages, so it is best to choose those that have been off the vine for a few months in order to yield sweeter soup.

While working as assistant tenzo at an East Coast Zen center, we served winter squash every day, as it was all we had left from our summer garden. After three months of this diet, all the monks had turned orange!

INGREDIENTS

2 tablespoons olive oil or butter
1 onion, peeled and sliced
1 large squash, peeled and cut into chunks, about 6 cups
Pinch of dried red pepper
1 tablespoon sugar
Approximately 4 cups water or vegetable stock
Salt
Handful chopped fresh mint

SERVES FOUR

- Heat the oil or butter in a heavy-based soup pot.
- Add the onions to the pot and sauté until golden. Then, add the squash, red pepper, and sugar and continue cooking until the pepper is softened.
- Add enough water or vegetable stock to cover. Bring to a boil and then simmer for about 1 hour.
- Remove from the heat and purée in a food processor.
- Adjust the salt to taste.
- Just before serving, garnish with the mint.

BROCCOLI WITH GARLIC

INGREDIENTS

2 or 3 large heads of broccoli
3 tablespoons olive oil
3 cloves garlic, peeled and chopped
Salt and pepper

SERVES FOUR

- Clean the heads of broccoli and cook them in a saucepan of boiling salted water for about 5 minutes. Drain and immediately plunge into cold water.
- Dry the broccoli on a paper towel and chop into small pieces.
- Heat the oil in a large sauté pan and add the chopped garlic. Sauté until coloured but not browned. Add the broccoli and sauté until the ingredients are heated thoroughly.
- Add salt and pepper to taste and serve.

SESAME FLATCAKES

These are a kind of tasty Asian pancake and they are great for soaking up soup.

Any pancake recipe will do if you omit the sugar, use sesame oil in place of regular oil, and add generous amounts of chopped scallions and sesame seeds. Here's the recipe I usually use.

INGREDIENTS

1½ cups unbleached flour
1½ teaspoons baking powder
1 teaspoon salt
1½ cups milk
3 tablespoons cold-pressed sesame oil, not toasted
2 large eggs
2 cups scallions, chopped
1 cup sesame seeds, toasted
Oil for cooking

SERVES FOUR

- Sift together the dry ingredients in a large bowl.
- In a separate bowl, whisk together the wet ingredients.
- Now, fold the dry ingredients into the wet ingredients until a batter is formed. Then, add the scallions and sesame seeds.
- Oil the griddle and place over the heat.
- Spoon a little of the batter onto the griddle so that a thin layer is formed.
- Cook until the underside is browned, then flip and brown the other side.
- Carefully remove from the griddle and serve immediately.

CURRIED ROAST POTATOES
WITH FRESH LIME

Curry paste is available in any Asian or Indian market. It's great to have around as it can liven up dishes and it's more flavorful than dried curry powder.

The important thing about this recipe is that the potatoes brown as they cook. Try heating the skillet before adding the potatoes or placing the sheet pan on the bottom of the oven, just above the heating element.

INGREDIENTS

2 pounds new potatoes, halved or quartered depending on size
2–3 teaspoons curry paste
2 tablespoons vegetable oil
Salt to taste
1 lime, juiced
Handful of fresh chopped cilantro to garnish

SERVES FOUR

- Preheat oven to 450°F (230°C).
- In a bowl, toss the potatoes with the curry paste, oil, and salt.
- Spread on a sheet pan or a cast-iron skillet and place in the oven. Roast for 45 minutes until the potatoes are tender, then remove from the oven.
- Transfer the potatoes onto a serving platter and sprinkle with fresh lime juice. Garnish with cilantro to serve.

An Axe through the Tongue

Color is like an awl in the eye.
Sound is like a stick in the ear.
Flavor is like an axe through
the tongue.

Yen Tsun

FRENCH LENTILS WITH FETA AND MINT

Tangy feta cheese and fresh mint combine to create a delicious and wholesome lentil-based dish.

I use a variety of different types of lentil for this dish, but my favorites are the small, green French lentils. They cook quickly and seem to have more flavor than most other lentils. This is a dish that really benefits from a good quality extra virgin olive oil.

INGREDIENTS

2 cups French lentils, picked over and rinsed
7 cups water
1 bay leaf
1 tablespoon extra virgin olive oil
1 cup crumbled feta cheese
Handful of fresh mint, torn into pieces
Salt and freshly ground pepper to taste
1 lemon, cut into wedges

SERVES FOUR

- Place the lentils, water, and bay leaf in a large saucepan.
- Bring to a boil, then reduce the heat and simmer for about 25 minutes or until the lentils are tender, but not falling apart.
- Drain the lentils thoroughly and toss with the olive oil in a bowl.
- Allow to cool for a few minutes, then add the feta, fresh mint, and salt and pepper to taste.
- Serve garnished with lemon wedges.

STEAMED RED CHARD WITH ROASTED PINE NUTS

Red chard is delicious and tender in this simple preparation. The pine nuts can be roasted in a heavy-based skillet on the stovetop, or you could spread them on a sheet pan and place them in a hot oven for a few minutes. Check them often; they turn from brown to burnt quickly.

INGREDIENTS

2 bunches red chard, leaves and stems chopped
Spray of extra virgin olive oil
Salt and pepper to taste
Handful of roasted pine nuts

SERVES FOUR

- Parboil the chard in a saucepan for about 2–3 minutes until just tender.
- Drain and spread on a platter. Using tongs, separate the leaves and spray with olive oil.
- Season with salt and pepper and garnish with the pine nuts to serve.

BROWN RICE WITH GOMASIO

Gomasio is a Japanese condiment made with toasted sesame seeds and salt, which are ground together in a suribachi—a special sort of mortar. If you can't find one, a regular mortar and pestle will do.

Ending up with a decent pot of fluffy brown rice may require experimentation. Don't check the rice during cooking; removing the lid releases the steam and drops the temperature. A pot with a tight-fitting lid is essential.

FOR THE RICE
2½ cups water
1 teaspoon salt
1 cup brown rice

FOR THE GOMASIO
1 cup sesame seeds
1 tablespoon sea salt
Optional: thinly sliced jalapeño pepper, to garnish
SERVES FOUR

- Place the water and salt in a heavy-based pot and bring to a boil.
- Add the rice and return to a boil.
- Stir once, then cover and simmer for about 40 minutes, or until the water has disappeared.
- To make the gomasio, toast the sesame seeds in a heavy-based skillet, stirring constantly.
- When the sesame seeds begin to brown, spread them out onto a sheet pan to cool.
- Grind the sesame seeds, a tablespoon or two at a time, with a few pinches of salt in a suribachi or in a mortar with a pestle until moist and grainy. The smell is indescribable! Adjust the quantity of salt to seeds, according to your own taste.
- When the rice is cooked, sprinkle over the gomasio and garnish with the jalapeño pepper, if using, and serve.

ADZUKI BEANS

Adzuki beans are small red beans popular in Japan and renowned in macrobiotic cooking for their health benefits. One traditional way to cook them is to start them on the stovetop in a stoneware pot, then finish them in a hot oven. This is a great way to cook any variety of dried bean, as the clay pot dramatically improves the flavor.

INGREDIENTS

2 cups adzuki beans, soaked overnight
1–2-inch piece of dried kombu (a type of seaweed)
½ teaspoon salt
A few snipped chives to garnish

SERVES FOUR

Zen Onions

Do not enter the meditation hall smelling of onions!

Dogen

- Place the soaked, drained beans into a soup pot.
- Add about 5 cups of water and bring to a boil, then reduce to a high simmer.
- Add the kombu and salt and continue cooking for about 1 hour until tender.
- Before serving, discard the kombu.
- Garnish with chives and serve.

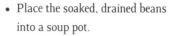

SPICY KALE WITH GARLIC AND TOMATOES

INGREDIENTS

1 tablespoon olive oil
1–2 cloves garlic, peeled and minced
½ jalapeño pepper, seeded and chopped
¼ dried ancho pepper, slivered
4 plum tomatoes, seeded and cut into wedges
1 large bunch kale, stems removed, leaves washed and torn

SERVES FOUR

- Heat the oil in a skillet and add the garlic, jalapeño, and ancho pepper. Sauté for a few minutes, then add the tomatoes and sauté for 10 minutes.
- Add the kale, reduce the heat and cook for a further 15 minutes, then serve.

HARBY'S TWICE-COOKED POLENTA

This is a twice-cooked polenta, first cooked as a cereal, cooled and cut into cakes, then baked. It has to cool for 1–2 hours before baking, but it can be prepared ahead of time.

INGREDIENTS

Oil for greasing
5 cups water or vegetable stock
1 teaspoon salt
1½ cups polenta (cornmeal)
2 tablespoons butter
½ cup grated Parmesan cheese

SERVES FOUR

- Preheat a broiler and lightly grease a 9 x 9-inch baking pan with the oil.
- In a saucepan, bring the water or stock to a boil. Add the salt, then slowly add the polenta, stirring constantly.
- Return to a boil, then lower the heat and continue cooking, stirring often to prevent the mixture sticking or forming lumps. It will take about 15 minutes for the polenta to soften and completely thicken.
- Remove from heat and pour into the oiled baking pan. Let the polenta cool completely in the pan, then using a spatula, divide it into equal squares.
- Gently lift out each square and arrange them on a sheet pan.
- Top each square with a pad of butter and a generous amount of Parmesan cheese. Place under the hot broiler for about 3–4 minutes or until heated and nicely browned.
- Serve warm.

DREAMING OF PORK HOCK

The ancient Taoist sage Chuang Tzu dreamed he was a butterfly fluttering among the trees. He awoke somewhat disconcerted and fell into wondering, "Was I just Chuang Tzu dreaming of a butterfly, or am I a butterfly dreaming of Chuang Tzu?"

I often wonder if I'm a smoked pork hock dreaming of a Cuban black bean soup. I ask myself, can there be Cuban black bean soup outside the realm of smoked pork?

CUBAN BLACK BEAN SOUP

This is not strictly Cuban black bean soup as I have eliminated the smoked pork. But, the following recipe is very satisfying all the same, especially if it is baked in a stoneware crock.

INGREDIENTS

3 tablespoons olive oil
1 large onion, peeled and chopped
1 celery stalk, chopped
2 carrots, peeled and diced
6 cloves garlic, peeled and minced
4 jalapeño peppers, seeded and chopped
1 pound dried black beans, soaked overnight
2 cups water or vegetable stock
1 bay leaf
2 teaspoons balsamic vinegar
2 tablespoons chopped fresh cilantro
Salt and pepper to taste
Optional toppings: diced red onion, sour cream, shredded Cheddar cheese

SERVES FOUR

- If you are using a stoneware crock, preheat the oven to 350°F (180°C).
- Heat 2 tablespoons of the oil in a soup pot or stoneware crock. Add the onion, celery, carrots, garlic, and peppers and sauté for about 10 minutes until soft.
- Drain and rinse the soaking black beans and add them to the pot along with the water or stock, the bay leaf, and the remaining olive oil.
- Bring to a boil, then reduce heat and simmer covered for about 2 hours. If you are using a stoneware crock, after the beans have come to a boil, cover the pot and place in the preheated oven for 2 hours. The beans will be softer and more flavorful the more slowly the soup is cooked.
- Check that the beans are tender, then remove about ⅓ of the soup and purée it in a food processor.
- Return the purée to the pot, add the vinegar and cilantro, and stir.
- Season to taste and serve topped with onions, sour cream or Cheddar cheese.

BRAISED ENDIVE WITH THYME

A heavy-based pan with a lid is vital for braising. A special braising pan has a lid with an inner layer of spikes that help moisture to circulate by inducing it to drip back onto the vegetables.

INGREDIENTS

2 tablespoons butter or olive oil
4 heads endive
1 shallot, peeled and chopped
2 sprigs fresh thyme
1 bay leaf
2 tablespoons water
Salt and pepper to taste

SERVES FOUR

- Heat the butter or oil in a pan. Add the endive, shallot, thyme, and bay leaf and sauté for a couple of minutes.
- Add the water, then reduce the heat and cover. Simmer for 20–25 minutes then check. If the endive is browned and fork-tender, it's done. If not, stir, re-cover, and cook until soft.
- Add salt and pepper to taste and serve.

LINGUINE WITH GREENS AND SEA VEGETABLE SAUCE

Recently, I made a big pot of greens with tomatoes and reduced the leftover water, or pot liquor as they call it in the South. The flavor reminded me of a clam sauce. The addition of some sea vegetables resulted in a pronounced, rich briny flavor.

INGREDIENTS

1 pound linguine
1 tablespoon olive oil
2 cloves garlic, peeled and minced
1 shallot, peeled and chopped
½ red or green jalapeño, seeded and minced
14-ounce can whole peeled tomatoes
1 large bunch of collard greens, stems removed, leaves washed and chopped
¼ cup dulce (seaweed)

SERVES FOUR

- Cook the linguine until al dente (see instructions on page 117).
- Heat the olive oil in a large soup pot, add the garlic, shallot, and jalapeño pepper and gently sauté until softened.
- Add the tomatoes with their juice and mash with a spoon or potato masher.
- Now, add the vegetable stock or water and bring to a boil.
- Once boiling, add the chopped collard greens and simmer for 45 minutes.
- Once cooked, remove and reserve the greens and whole tomatoes, but leave the broth.
- Snip dried pieces of seaweed into the pot with a pair of scissors—dulce, the purple seaweed from the North Atlantic, works well. Reduce the liquid over high heat for about 15 minutes until you have a slightly thickened, intensely flavored broth.
- Toss the broth with reserved greens, tomatoes, and cooked linguine and serve immediately.

Cold Mountain

Living in the mountains,
mind ill at ease,
all I do is grieve at the passing years.
At great labor I gathered the
herbs of long life,
but has all my striving made
me an immortal?
My garden is broad and wrapped
now in clouds,
but the woods are bright
and the moon is full.
What am I doing here?
Why don't I go home?
I'm bound by the spell of the
cinnamon trees!

Han-Shuan

° Translated by Burton Watson

CAULIFLOWER WITH MUSTARD CREAM

INGREDIENTS

1 large head of cauliflower
1 teaspoon butter
1 shallot, peeled and finely chopped
1 cup heavy cream
1 teaspoon Dijon mustard
2 teaspoons capers
Garnish with chopped fresh summer savory, if available

SERVES FOUR

- Bring a large pot of salted water to a boil and add the cauliflower.
- Bring back to a boil, then reduce the heat and simmer the cauliflower for about 10–15 minutes until you can easily penetrate its core with a knife. Remove from the pot and drain.
- When it's cool enough to handle, cut the cauliflower into florets and set aside.
- Heat the butter in a saucepan, add the shallot, and sauté until browned.
- Add the cream and cook until the liquid has reduced by half.
- Swirl in mustard, then add the cauliflower and capers.
- Cook for a few more minutes, then add salt and pepper to taste and garnish with a teaspoon of savory.

GRATED BEET SALAD WITH APPLE

This salad works best with small young beets. I don't specify exactly how much balsamic vinegar to use because beets seem to be able to take a lot.

INGREDIENTS

2 medium-sized Granny Smith apples, peeled and coarsely grated
2 medium-sized raw beets, peeled and grated
1 clove garlic, peeled and minced
Balsamic vinegar to taste
Extra virgin olive oil
Salt to taste

SERVES FOUR

- Put the grated apples and beets in a bowl and toss with the garlic and balsamic vinegar.
- Drizzle with the oil and season to taste before serving.

ROASTED VEGETABLE
LASAGNA

Lasagna seems to benefit from being cooked a day ahead of time, then reheated again before serving. Most leftover vegetables work well in this dish, as does a layer of puréed pulses. The following recipe calls for roasted vegetables and mozzarella which makes a lighter, fresher tasting dish.

INGREDIENTS

Oil for greasing
6 Japanese eggplants, halved lengthwise
2 large Portobello mushrooms, cut into chunks
1 large red bell pepper, peeled, sliced and seeded
2 tablespoons salt
1 pound lasagna noodles
4 cups tomato sauce (see recipe on page 50)
¼ pound fresh mozzarella, thinly sliced
½ pound ricotta cheese
4 tablespoons grated Parmesan cheese

SERVES SIX TO EIGHT

- Preheat oven to 375°F (190°C) and lightly oil a 9 x 12-inch baking pan.
- Roast the eggplant, mushrooms, and pepper. They can be grilled, dry-roasted in a pan on the stovetop, or sprayed with olive oil and roasted in a hot oven. Set aside.
- Bring a large pot of salty water to a boil and cook the lasagna noodles in batches. They take about 4 minutes to cook until soft but not floppy (if you can fold the cooked sheet of lasagna in half, then it is overcooked). Plunge into cold water immediately after cooking, then drain thoroughly.
- Now, layer the oiled baking pan first with a ladle-full of tomato sauce, then a layer of pasta, then the roasted vegetables, then another ladle-full of tomato sauce, and then the mozzarella and ricotta. Keep layering until you have about four layers of pasta and end with a layer tomato sauce. Sprinkle the top with grated Parmesan cheese and any leftover vegetables.
- Cover the pan first with a layer of plastic wrap, then a layer of aluminum foil. It's important that the pan be tightly sealed so that the noodles continue cooking without drying out.
- Bake in the oven for 45 minutes, then remove the foil and plastic wrap. Return the baking pan to the oven and bake for another 15 minutes to brown the top. If the lasagna is to be reheated later, don't remove the plastic and foil. Reheat the covered lasagna in a 325°F (170°C) oven until warmed through.
- Remove from the oven and let it stand for 15 minutes before serving.

WARM SAVOY CABBAGE WITH FRESH SAGE

Savoy cabbage has a more delicate flavor and texture than regular green cabbage.

INGREDIENTS

1 large head Savoy cabbage
3 tablespoons butter or olive oil
2 shallots, peeled and finely chopped
2 cloves garlic, peeled and finely chopped
15 leaves fresh sage, chopped
Salt and pepper to taste

SERVES SIX TO EIGHT

- Cut the cabbage in half and remove the core. Place the halves into a large pan of boiling salted water and cook for 5 minutes. Drain and cool.
- Once cool enough to handle, cut the cabbage into large chunks.
- Heat the oil or butter in a skillet and add the chopped shallots and garlic. Sauté for a few minutes, then add the cabbage leaves. Sauté until tender.
- Add the sage and season with salt and pepper before serving.

RUTABAGA, LEEK, AND SWEET POTATO PUREE

INGREDIENTS

1½ pounds rutabaga, peeled and chopped into cherry-sized chunks
1½ pounds sweet potato, peeled and chopped the same as above
3 tablespoons olive oil
3 leeks, washed and chopped
1½ teaspoons chopped fresh rosemary
Salt and pepper to taste

SERVES SIX TO EIGHT

- Cook the rutabaga and sweet potato in a saucepan of boiling water and cook for about 15 minutes until fork-tender. Drain, reserving the cooking water.
- Heat 1 tablespoon of the olive oil in a skillet and add the leeks and rosemary. Sauté for about 5 minutes until the leeks are soft.
- Place the rutabaga, sweet potato and leeks in a food processor and purée, adding the remaining olive oil and, if needed, a little cooking water. It should be the consistency of mashed potatoes.
- Add salt and pepper to taste and serve.

Sweet Potato

Of all things living I'd be a sweet potato, fresh dug up.

Shinkichi Takahashi

Translated by Lucian Stryk

MISO SOUP

Miso is a purée of soybeans and wheat, barley or rice. It is protein-rich and an essential ingredient in Japanese cooking. The most immediate form of miso soup is to simply strain miso into hot water. Miso can also be added to most any soup that will benefit from its earthy and slightly tangy flavor. I use it when I find a vegetable soup needs a little more body. Miso seems to keep forever in the refrigerator but it actually loses its flavor after a few months. The same goes for cooked miso soup, which only keeps for a couple of days in the refrigerator.

What follows is a basic miso recipe. The flavor of the finished soup depends a lot on the stock. Here I use dashi, *a Japanese form of prepared vegetable stock, usually containing fish. It often comes in the form of a tea bag, which is boiled to produce a soup base.*

INGREDIENTS

4 dried shiitake mushrooms
5 cups dashi or vegetable stock
1 teaspoon vegetable oil
hallots, peeled and finely chopped
1 carrot, peeled and thinly sliced
¼ cup daikon, cut into small cubes
2 teaspoons sake
3–4 teaspoons miso paste
Soy sauce to taste
3 scallions, chopped
Half sheet of nori, crumpled for garnish

SERVES FOUR

- Place the shiitake mushrooms in a bowl with boiling water and let them soak for 10 minutes. Drain, and save the water. Rinse again and slice thinly.
- Pour the reserved mushroom water through a coffee filter and add to the dashi or stock.
- Heat the oil in a soup pot and add shallots and mushrooms. Sauté for 1–2 minutes. Add the carrots, daikon and sake.
- Reduce the liquid slightly then add the dashi or stock.
- Bring to a boil, then reduce the heat and simmer for about 5–6 minutes until the carrots and daikon are tender.
- Scoop out about a cup of broth and stir in the miso paste. If the miso is unpasteurized, strain the mixture. Add this to the soup and reduce the heat. Miso shouldn't be boiled. Taste and, if needed, flavor with soy sauce.
- Serve garnished with chopped scallions and crumpled nori.

KASHA WITH VEGETABLES

Kasha *is the Russian term for toasted buckwheat groats. I use whole groats for this dish, as opposed to cracked, and cook them in the manner of Italian risotto: uncovered and adding stock gradually until absorbed.*

INGREDIENTS

2 tablespoons olive oil
1 onion, peeled and finely chopped
1 carrot, peeled and finely chopped
1 clove garlic, peeled and finely chopped
2 Portobello mushrooms, sliced
1 stalk celery, finely chopped
3 cups kasha
½ cup dry white wine
About 2 pints hot vegetable stock or water
1 beet, steamed until tender and sliced
A few sprigs of fresh parsley
Crumbled goat cheese or a dollop of sour cream to garnish

SERVES FOUR

- Heat the oil in a large skillet or soup pot. Add the onion, carrot, garlic, mushrooms, and celery and sauté until brown. Add the kasha and heat for another 2–3 minutes. Add the wine and continue stirring until it has all been absorbed by the kasha.
- Gradually add cups of hot vegetable stock or water. Simmer, stirring occasionally for about 20 minutes. The kasha quickly absorbs the liquid and should be soft and chewy.
- Toss in the beets and remove from the heat. Serve topped with parsley, goat cheese, or a dollop of sour cream.

POACHED PEARS

INGREDIENTS

4 large ripe pears, peeled, cored, and halved
1 bottle red wine
1 cinnamon stick
½ cup of sugar
Fresh mint leaves to garnish

SERVES FOUR

- Place the pears in a heavy-based saucepan and add enough red wine to cover them. Bring to a boil, then add the cinnamon stick.
- Reduce the heat and simmer for about 10 minutes until the pears are softened. Remove and transfer them to a dish.
- Bring the wine back to a boil, add the sugar, and boil until reduced. Spoon over the pears and garnish with mint.

This hut is larger than the earth since there's nothing that is not.
In the small charcoal stove burn sun and countless stars,
and the corners of the kitchen buzz with humankind.

The Kitchen

In my tenure as tenzo, my taste in food has certainly changed. Except for a few years during which I ate macrobiotically, I'm not a vegetarian and neither are most of the people I cook for. But at the Zen Center we adhere to a vegetarian diet. Letting go of meat as the cornerstone of a satisfying meal has been a challenge. Once in a while I'll fire up my grill and cook a piece of fish or roast a chicken, but unless it's a special occasion, there is a feeling of guilt which makes it hard to really enjoy it.

When I first began to cook at the Zen Center, I often tried to fill the meat void with bulk. I thought eating heavy, oily vegetables and dairy products was the only way to approach the level of satisfaction most gain from eating meat. Gradually my approach has changed. Light, simple food is really the best approach when most of your customers are spending up to nine hours a day sitting absolutely still.

TOM PAPPAS

METHODS AND INGREDIENTS

All the three-bowl menus in this book are balanced for both nutrition and taste. But Tom's recipes are meant to inspire as well as instruct. We hope you will mix and match, and experiment with other ingredients. Try adapting some of Tom's methods to work with some of your own favorite foods. We hope this book is just the beginning of a new way of cooking for you. In these pages we've listed some of the staples of our own kitchens. These are the foods we come back to again and again.

Very few of the recipes require special ingredients. The most difficult to find may be umeboshi paste (see recipe on page 27) and seaweed. But, what with the wonders of the global village, city-dwellers at least should be able to find these in health food or Asian markets.

Part of the experience of Zen is to bring sacredness and beauty into the everyday. If you can achieve Zen cooking in your own kitchen, then why not try a little Zen shopping too. Transform what used to be a chore into an experience of nowness.

PANTRY ESSENTIALS

The kitchen is a workplace and needs to be clean and tidy. You should have essential ingredients in stock and they should be easy to get at and easy to put away. Throw out items you have been saving "just in case" and discard any dried goods that you have had for more than six months.

Oils (Preferably cold-pressed) olive oil; a neutral oil such as peanut or sunflower; sesame and safflower oil

Dried herbs Oregano, mint, bay leaves, basil, thyme, rosemary, sage

Spices (Preferably whole seeds) black pepper, cumin, coriander, cinnamon, turmeric, sea salt, curry powder, cayenne, mustard seeds, caraway, cloves, allspice

Vinegars Organic cider vinegar, rice wine vinegar, wine vinegar

Flavorings Naturally fermented soy sauce (shoyu), hot pepper sauce, fresh ginger and garlic, vegetable stock cubes, tahini, peanut butter, creamed coconut, miso, honey

Grains Long-grain brown and white rice, 100 percent wholemeal flour (stoneground), 81 percent wholemeal flour, strong white flour, bulgur wheat, couscous, dried pasta, red and brown lentils, chickpeas, red beans, your own favorite grains and beans

Canned goods Plum tomatoes, chickpeas, red beans, sweetcorn, tomato purée

Bottled goods Olives, mustard, chutney

Nuts and seeds Sesame and sunflower seeds, pine nuts

Weekly store Natural yogurt, lemons, milk, cheese, fresh basil, beancurd, eggs

Grains and Seeds

Grains and Seeds These provide the staple foods for most of the world's population, since cereal grains, either whole or as flour products, are excellent, well-balanced, complete sources of nutrients. The trick is to cook them properly. There's nothing more dispiriting than undercooked rice, or porridge that's been boiled to sludge. Follow our tips and take care. Cooking grains well means paying attention—another opportunity to practice a little Zen.

Bulgur wheat This is parboiled, cracked wheat. Although relatively unknown in the West, it is the staple food of many Middle Eastern countries, where it is served mixed with rice and used as the basis for cold salads.

Barley Whole barley or pot barley is more nutritious than the refined pearl barley, but it takes longer to cook. It's useful for soups, stews, and casseroles.

Buckwheat Not strictly a grain but the seed of a herbaceous plant, buckwheat is popular in Russia and other Eastern European countries.

Kasha, as it is also called, loses some flavor if it is not dry roasted before cooking (see recipe on page 111).

Corn (maize) Wholegrain maize or cornmeal retains all the goodness of the corn. Stoneground is the best if you can obtain it. Polenta is the Italian name for yellow maize or cornmeal (see recipes for cornbread and polenta on pages 28 and 84).

Oats These are a rich source of nutrients. They are usually used only in breakfast cereals, but can also be added to soups, stews, and other savory dishes. Oatmeal flour is good in bread and cake making.

Rice This is an excellent food for the cook. It is versatile and once you have learned to judge how to cook it well, you can produce good plain boiled rice and rice-combination dishes without fail. Before it is cooked, rice should be washed. American or European-packed rice only needs a light rinse, but loose rice or Asian-packed rice should be rinsed in a colander until the water stops running milky.

GENERAL RULES FOR COOKING GRAINS

Rinse the grains under cold water and drain. Measure the cooking water into the pot and bring to a boil. Add the grain, stir, add salt if you wish (about ½ teaspoon to 8 ounces of grains), and return the pot to a boil. Reduce heat to very low. Cover and cook until the water is absorbed and the grain is tender.

COOKING TIPS

- Do not stir grains during cooking; it makes them sticky.
- For a change, sauté the grains with chopped onion in a little oil before adding the cooking water. It changes their flavor.
- Cook lentils and brown rice together.
- Combine leftover grains with beans, add a dressing and chopped salad vegetables.
- Add herbs or spices to the grain cooking water.

Brown rice This is more nutritious than white rice and if you enjoy the flavor, and also have the extra time needed to cook it, then you will benefit from including it in your diet. It takes nearly 50 percent longer to cook than white rice, however, and if you get it wrong, the results can be unappetizing. But the taste complements some dishes perfectly, such as Spicy Squash Stew with Peppers (see recipe on page 40) or Tomato and Pan-roasted Vegetable Sauce (see recipe on page 72).

Long-grain rice This type of rice remains in separate grains and turns light and fluffy when cooked. It is ideal with almost any main dish.

Short-grain rice This goes soft when cooked and the grains tend to stick to one another. It is ideal for risottos and puddings.

Wild rice This is a cereal grain native to North America, China, and Japan. It's in the same family as the rice plant, but it has never been domestically cultivated. When cooked, it has a delicate nutty flavor.

Semolina (couscous) This is produced from the starchy endosperm of the wheat grain. It is milled in various grades to give fine, medium or coarse semolina. Fine semolina is used in puddings and pasta, while coarse semolina is used to make couscous (see recipe on page 76).

Nuts and Seeds In general,
nuts and seeds are delicious and nutritious foods, whether eaten raw on their own or used as part of a recipe. To blanch nuts, put them in a pan of boiling water and allow to stand for 2–3 minutes (longer for hazelnuts and cobnuts). Drain, rinse in cold water, and rub off the skins.

Pasta Italian-style pasta is made
from a dough of wheat flour, eggs and water. The dough is rolled out and cut into a variety of shapes, then dried before cooking in water. The best pasta is made from hard-grained wheat, particularly durum wheat. We keep a variety on hand. It's our staple fast food. We won't dictate which shapes to use. Suffice it to say—experiment.

GENERAL RULES FOR COOKING PASTA

When cooking dried or fresh pasta, the important rule is to use a large pot and plenty of water. Generally 1 pound of pasta needs 6 pints of water and about 1 tablespoon of salt, which should be added after the water has been boiled and before the pasta goes in. To prevent the pasta sticking to itself during cooking, a little butter or oil can be added to the water. Thus, bring the water to a rolling boil, add the salt, and 2 tablespoons of butter or oil and then carefully feed the pasta into the pot. Boil the pasta, uncovered, until it is soft on the outside but with a slight resistance at the center, this is known as *al dente*. Cooking times vary depending on the type of pasta and whether it is bought dried or fresh, or if it is homemade.

Beans and bean sprouts

Beans are an important part of a vegetarian diet since they provide protein which vegetarians often find they lack. But beans contain two starches that are difficult to digest if they are not broken down before eating. So it is essential that they are thoroughly pre-soaked and cooked for the correct time (see box, right). Strictly speaking, lentils and split peas do not require soaking, but if you do soak them it doesn't do any harm. We often cook double and store the extra in the refrigerator. They keep best if only lightly covered for four to five days.

When beans or other seeds, such as alfalfa, are sprouted, their nutritional value increases. They are also quick, simple and cheap to grow and available all year round. Mung bean sprouts are the most popular commercial variety, and the bean sprouts we are most familiar with in Chinese restaurant dishes. Other non-commercial favorites are sprouted chickpeas, kidney beans, soybeans, and lentils. Mixtures of beans may also be sprouted. Adzuki beans, lentils, chickpeas, and mung beans are a popular mix. Wholegrains such as rice, wheat, and oats can also be sprouted, but they should be briefly cooked by stir-frying or steaming before eating. Fenugreek, alfalfa, sunflower, and sesame seeds all work well.

Apart from fresh in salads or in stir-fry dishes, bean sprouts are good in soups and casseroles, wrapped in thin phyllo pastry sheets (as in spring rolls and samosas) or gently chopped in a food processor and added to bread dough before baking.

They're simple to grow and it'll take you back to your school days in the science lab. Soak the beans for a day. Then spread them over a sheet of damp paper towel on a tray. Put them in a dark cupboard and wait a few days; three should do it, and then you'll have some healthy, crunchy homegrown vegetables.

Soybean products

Miso A fermented soybean and grain product that has a thick consistency and is usually dark-colored with a pungent smell. Miso is rich in vitamins (including B_{12}) and minerals and is good for settling the digestive system.

GENERAL RULES FOR COOKING BEANS

Soaking method Remove grit, stones, or odd-looking beans, then cover in cold water; 2 pints per 8 ounces of beans. Leave to soak for 8–10 hours, then cook. If the beans are cooked in the water they are soaked in, the water will be completely absorbed by the end of the cooking time and the beans will not need to be drained. This method preserves any vitamins.

COOKING TIPS

- Dried beans expand from twice to 2½ times their normal volume when cooked.
- Do not add salt to the beans until the end of the cooking time.
- Do not discard any water in which beans have been cooked as it makes excellent stock.
- Chickpeas and red beans foam when first cooked. Remove the foam after 20 or 30 minutes.

Tom uses it in soups, stews, stocks, sauces, dressings, dips, and spreads. It is salty, so do not add extra salt.

Soy sauce This sauce is an all-purpose seasoning used to highlight the individual flavor of all the ingredients in a dish. It should not be used to drown the flavor of food. Shoyu is soy sauce made from a fermented soybean and wheat mixture while tamari is made only from soybeans and is gluten-free.

Tofu This has got to be one of the handiest foods for someone on a vegetarian diet. Tofu is rich in protein and minerals and low in fat. It's versatile and, when treated with care, it's tasty (see recipe on page 87). Tofu is made by boiling soybeans, mashing the boiled beans through a sieve and collecting the liquid or milk, which is then set using a coagulant. Excess water is pressed off (see box, below). Fresh tofu is best kept in water and stored in the refrigerator.

HOMEMADE TOFU

- Cover 1 pound soybeans with water and leave to soak for at least 12 hours.
- Change the water once during soaking.
- Drain and grind the beans either in an electric grinder or hand mill.
- Transfer to a heavy pan and add twice as much water by volume as beans.
- Bring to a boil, reduce heat and simmer for 1 hour.
- Arrange three to four layers of cheesecloth inside a colander placed over a large bowl or pan.
- Drain the bean mixture through this.
- Finally, gather the cheesecloth around the collected bean pulp and squeeze out as much of the remaining liquid into the bowl or pan as possible.
- Transfer the collected liquid to a glass bowl.

- Add 3 tablespoons fresh lemon juice to it, stir once, cover with a damp cloth and leave in a warm spot (80°F (120°C) is perfect) for 8–12 hours or until the beancurd sets.
- Drain through cheesecloth to remove excess liquid. The beancurd may now be used.
- For a professional look, pour it into a square mold, put a light weight on top and press for 4 hours. Remove the weight, pour over some water, cover and store in a refrigerator.
- For flavored beancurd, simmer a block or small squares of it in oil and soy sauce with mint or garlic, nutmeg, cinnamon, cloves, fennel or black pepper, or whatever seasoning you wish.

Vegetables

These are at the heart of this book. Treat your vegetables with respect: buy them fresh, wash them tenderly, cook them with care and attention—and they will reward your palate with an explosion of flavor and texture.

Always wash vegetables thoroughly and where suitable give them a good scrub. Peel them only if strictly necessary, since the skin contains many nutrients and is often very tasty.

As a rule, cook vegetables in the minimum amount of time needed. The intention is to ensure they retain their color and texture. Tom likes to pan-roast vegetables for maximum intensity of flavor. You need a big cast-iron skillet to do this well. The more use it's had, the better. The cast-iron pans Tom uses at the Center are so big they fit over two burners.

- Use your discretion when deciding how much to chop your vegetables for pan roasting. For example, small Japanese eggplants can be cooked whole, whereas carrots are best if chopped into matchsticks before cooking.
- Heat the pan as hot as it will safely go.
- Add the minimum of oil. Add none at all if your pan is well seasoned.
- Throw in the vegetables and toss as for stir-frying.

This method of cooking gives the vegetables great integrity of flavor. If you're not cooking them this way, boiling them in the minimum amount of water necessary will help retain flavor and nutrients.

Root vegetables

Carrots, potatoes and the like are best cooked at a fast simmer/slow boil to retain as much flavor as possible, but you don't want to have the heat so high that the water is violently agitated, causing the outer parts of the vegetables to disintegrate before the food is cooked at the center. For best results, put the root vegetables in three times their volume of cold water, place the lid on the pan and bring swiftly to a boil. Then reduce the heat.

Green vegetables

Green beans, broccoli, and other green vegetables are exceptional in that they are best cooked in an open pan at a rolling boil. You must then serve them immediately or, if they are for a salad, chill them under a cold tap or plunge them into iced water until they are quite cold.

When cooking in this manner note the following points:

- The vegetables are normally cooked in salted water because the salt raises the temperature of boiling water a little.
- Have only about 1 inch of water in your pan. There should not be enough water in the pan for the vegetables to move around and break up.
- Have the water at a rolling boil before you put in the vegetables and maintain it that way.
- Use a large-based pan and do not overcrowd.

Tender leaf vegetables

Vegetables such as spinach are best cooked by washing well, shaking off the excess water, and cooking without any additional water over moderate heat, in a covered pan.

SEASONAL BUYING

Certain fruits, vegetables, and herbs both home-grown and imported, are particularly worth looking out for in each season:

Spring Asparagus, avocados, baby white turnips, bananas, beet, calabrese, chicory, citrus fruits, cucumbers, curly endive, green beans, mint, new potatoes, parsley, pineapples, radishes, snow peas, tomatoes, watercress, zucchini

Summer All types of lettuce, apples, beet, broccoli, carrots, cauliflower, celery, corn on the cob, eggplant, fava beans, French beans, garden peas, garlic, globe artichokes, Italian fennel, Italian plum tomatoes, kidney beans, bell peppers, runner beans, Spanish onions, tomatoes, watercress, zucchini

Fall All root crops, apples, avocados, basil, cabbage (drumhead), celery, chicory, chilies, Chinese cabbage, cucumbers, dates (fresh), endive, fennel, flageolet beans, French beans, grapes, kiwi fruit, pomegranates, red pepper, runner beans, shallots, spinach, corn on the cob, tomatoes, watercress, zucchini

Winter Avocados, beet, broccoli (purple/white), cabbage (red/white), carrots, calabrese, cauliflower, celery, chicory, coriander, endive, French beans, leeks, lemons, lettuce (iceberg or Cos), new potatoes, oranges, parsley, potatoes, snow peas

Fruit What with modern methods of artificial ripening, it's often hard to know just how fresh and ripe the fruit you're buying is. Bluntly, there's no substitute for fruit that's in season, but we all have to compromise sometimes.

Try to eat your fruit raw to take full advantage of its abundant vitamin C. To retain its nutritional value, keep cooking to a minimum.

Fruit is traditionally cooked by poaching in a sugar syrup. The slow cooking prevents the fruit from breaking up and the strong sugar solution prevents the fruit flavors and natural sugars leaking away, as would happen if you cooked the fruit in water. Poaching fruit in syrup may preserve the flavor, but at the expense of consuming hefty doses of sugar. Rather than poaching (or stewing in even the minimum of water) try baking or steaming fruit in its skin (see recipe on page 95).

Dried Fruit These are a very useful ingredient in a vegetarian diet since they contain all the goodness of fresh fruit in a concentrated form. They are an excellent addition in savory stuffings, casseroles, rice dishes, soups, and sauces.

Where there is a choice, buy the sun-dried varieties (or second best, freeze-dried) rather than those dried by artificial heating. Dried fruits will keep for up to a year or even longer if you deep-freeze them.

Eggs and Dairy If you are on a vegetarian regime, eating sufficient protein can be a problem. This is where eggs and dairy produce really can make a difference since they're both rich in protein. But you shouldn't rely on them too much because they're also hard to digest.

Eggs These contain high quality protein and cholesterol. Cholesterol-rich diets have recently been linked to heart disease, but in small amounts cholesterol is an essential nutrient; so including a few eggs in your diet is a good idea. Free-range eggs are very tasty but organic eggs taste best of all.

Cheese Apart from being a delicious food and a versatile ingredient for the cook, cheese is also relatively high in protein and a good source of the mineral calcium and Vitamins A and D. As with other dairy products, it also has a fairly high saturated fat content so it should be eaten in moderation and, where suitable, low-fat varieties should be used for cooking.

Dishes that contain cheese should not be overcooked or overheated. Under such conditions, some cheeses, particularly the hard varieties, become rubbery and difficult to digest.

Yogurt This is an excellent food. It is nourishing, good for the digestion and a versatile ingredient. Yogurt also has the reputation of promoting longevity and of being a good stamina food. It may be used in the preparation of soups and salads as a marinating agent, in entrées and in desserts, and even as a summer drink mixed with water, a pinch of salt and mint. Of course, it's delicious for breakfast mixed with tropical fruit or muesli (see recipes on pages 26 and 48).

Homemade yogurt is easy to prepare and is much fresher and more economical than most of the shop-bought varieties (see opposite).

MAKING YOGURT

- Place 1–2 pints of fresh milk (depending on how much you want to make) in a clean saucepan and bring to a boil. As soon as it bubbles, switch off the heat and transfer the milk to a clean ceramic or glass bowl.
- Allow the milk to cool to about blood temperature (98–100°F). To test, put your finger into the milk, which should be comfortably warm. If you like, use a thermometer, although we never do.
- Now stir in 1–2 tablespoons of live yogurt, cover with a lid and wrap the whole thing in a thick towel. Store in a warm place, above the hot area at the back of the refrigerator, for example, or in the sun or by a radiator; you can also pour it into a thermos.
- Leave to set for 10–12 hours, when the yogurt will be ready. Remove the towel and store in the refrigerator.
- For a thick yogurt, add 1–2 tablespoons of powdered milk to the fresh milk before starting. If you want to make a lot of yogurt, make it in several smaller batches rather than in one huge one.
- Your first attempt at yogurt-making may produce quite a thin, runny yogurt. Don't worry—it will get thicker as your own live yogurt starter improves.

INDEX

CARROLL & BROWN would like to thank:

Production manager
Karol Davies

Production assistant
Clair Reynolds

IT management
Elisa Merino

Picture research
Richard Soar

Index
Madeline Weston

Geoffrey Chesler for his input and enthusiasm.

We would also like to thank the Yokoji Zen Mountain Center, San Jacinto, for all their co-operation and for kindly allowing us to reproduce the images on pages 8 and 13.

Picture credits
Tony Stone Images page 15 and Robert Harding Picture Library page 21.

All food photography © Carroll & Brown.

Dave Scott would like to thank:

The many Zen cooks (*tenzo*) who over many years have given their skill, energy, and dedication to providing the nourishment that has sustained myself and all the other Zen practitioners with whom I have shared *sesshin* over the years.

Tom Pappas for his wonderful recipes and the down-to-earth Zen humor that had me laughing out loud when I first read his section of the manuscript.

Tenshin Fletcher Sensei for his teaching and friendship and for the wisdom and enormous commitment of energy and spirit that he has contributed to create and sustain Zen Mountain Center as a teaching monastery.

Genpo Merzel Roshi, Abbot, Kanzeon Sangha, who introduced me to Zen practice, who continues to support me in it, and who changed my life.

This book is dedicated to my family.

Tom Pappas would like to thank:

Kelly Spalding, and Sarah Maclean, who helped prepare the manuscript.

The staff and residents of the Zen Mountain Center.

FOR DETAILS OF THE ZEN MOUNTAIN CENTER CONTACT:

Yokoji Zen Mountain Center
P.O. Box 43, Mountain Center, CA 92561

Tel: (909) 659 5272
Fax: (909) 659 3275

email: zmc@primenet.com
website: http://www.zmc.org/zmc

ACKNOWLEDGMENTS